NIGHTMARE AT THE NIGHTCLUB
SPIDER-GWEN:
GHOST-SPIDER
IMPOSSIBLE YEAR

PREVIOUSLY

GWEN STACY OF EARTH-65 IS THE ONLY SPIDER ABLE TO TRAVERSE THE MULTIVERSE, BUT IN THE AFTERMATH OF SPIDER-GEDDON AND THE LOSS OF A FEW CLOSE FRIENDS, ALL GWEN WANTS TO DO IS GATHER HER FRIENDS AND FAMILY CLOSE.

WITH THAT MENTALITY, GWEN HAS TURNED HER ATTENTION TO BUILDING UP OLD FRIENDSHIPS AND EMBRACING HER ROLE AS SPIDER-WOMAN. BUT BEING A TEENAGE SUPER HERO COMES WITH NOT ONLY GREAT POWER AND RESPONSIBILITY, BUT GREAT COMPLICATIONS AS WELL...

GWEN STACY CREATED BY
STAN LEE & STEVE DITKO

COLLECTION EDITOR JENNIFER GRÜNWALD
ASSISTANT EDITOR CAITLIN O'CONNELL
ASSOCIATE MANAGING EDITOR KATERI WOODY
EDITOR, SPECIAL PROJECTS MARK D. BEAZLEY
VP PRODUCTION & SPECIAL PROJECTS JEFF YOUNGQUIST
BOOK DESIGNER STACIE ZUCKER

SVP PRINT, SALES & MARKETING DAVID GABRIEL
DIRECTOR, LICENSED PUBLISHING SVEN LARSEN
EDITOR IN CHIEF C.B. CEBULSKI
CHIEF CREATIVE OFFICER JOE QUESADA
PRESIDENT DAN BUCKLEY
EXECUTIVE PRODUCER ALAN FINE

SPIDER-GWEN: GHOST-SPIDER VOL. 2 — IMPOSSIBLE YEAR. Contains material originally published in magazine form as SPIDER-GWEN: GHOST SPIDER #5-10. First printing 2019. ISBN 978-1-302-91477-6. Published by MARVEL WORLDWIDE, INC., a subsidiary of MARVEL ENTERTAINMENT, LLC. OFFICE OF PUBLICATION: 135 West 50th Street, New York, NY 10020. © 2019 MARVEL No similarity between any of the names, characters, persons, and/or institutions in this magazine with those of any living or dead person or institution is intended, and any such similarity which may exist is purely coincidental. **Printed in Canada.** DAN BUCKLEY, President, Marvel Entertainment; JOHN NEE, Publisher; JOE QUESADA, Chief Creative Officer; TOM BREVOORT, SVP of Publishing; DAVID BOGART, Associate Publisher & SVP of Talent Affairs; DAVID GABRIEL, SVP of Sales & Marketing, Publishing; JEFF YOUNGQUIST, VP of Production & Special Projects; DAN CARR, Executive Director of Publishing Technology; ALEX MORALES, Director of Publishing Operations; DAN EDINGTON, Managing Editor; SUSAN CRESPI, Production Manager; STAN LEE, Chairman Emeritus. For information regarding advertising in Marvel Comics or on Marvel.com, please contact Vit DeBellis, Custom Solutions & Integrated Advertising Manager, at vdebellis@marvel.com. For Marvel subscription inquiries, please call 888-511-5480. **Manufactured between 7/12/2019 and 8/13/2019 by SOLISCO PRINTERS, SCOTT, QC, CANADA.**

10 9 8 7 6 5 4 3 2 1

IMPOSSIBLE YEAR

SEANAN McGUIRE
WRITER

TAKESHI MIYAZAWA
WITH ROSI KÄMPE (#10)
ARTISTS

IAN HERRING
COLOR ARTIST

VC's CLAYTON COWLES
LETTERER

BENGAL
COVER ART

KATHLEEN WISNESKI, LAUREN AMARO & DANNY KHAZEM
ASSISTANT EDITORS

DEVIN LEWIS
EDITOR

NICK LOWE
EXECUTIVE EDITOR

ONE! TWO!
ONE-TWO-THREE-FOUR!
YOU SAY YOU GOT RESPONSIBILITIES.
THAT MEANS YOU CAN'T JUST RUN AROUND WITH ME.
BABY, BABY, I SAY THAT YOU BETTER SLOW DOWN--
--STOP SWINGING YOUR WAY ALL OVER TOWN.
THIS IS NOT A CALL YOU CAN REFUSE.
PICK ME, PICK ME, OR YOU'RE GOING TO LOSE.
MARY JANES
Mary Janes

I'M GWEN STACY, AND I'M SO *VAIN* I DEFINITELY THINK THIS SONG IS ABOUT *ME*.

MJ IS MANY THINGS, BUT SHE'S NOT *SUBTLE*.

PICK ME UP, **PICK ME UP,** WON'T GET A SECOND CHANCE.

PICK ME UP, **PICK ME UP,** AT A WILD ROMANCE.

PICK ME UP, **PICK ME UP,** IS NO EXCHANGE FOR ME!

PICK ME UP, **PICK ME UP,** RESPONSIBILITY.

GREAT REHEARSAL, EVERYONE! GWEN, YOU WERE A LITTLE BEHIND THE BEAT.

MARY JANE "MJ" WATSON. LEAD SINGER, LEAD GUITARIST, LEAD PAIN IN THE NECK.

WHY IS IT ALWAYS "GWEN, YOU'RE BEHIND THE BEAT" AND NOT "I WAS RUSHING THE BEAT"?

I'M YOUR **DRUMMER.** THE BEAT IS LITERALLY MY **JOB.**

I KNOW WHAT I HEARD.

DON'T BE MEAN.

GLORY GRANT. KILLER ON THE KEYS. VOICE OF REASON.

THEY CAN DO THIS ALL NIGHT.
WE CAN SNEAK OUT. GET FOOD.
I AM AWARE.
I COULD GO FOR A CORN DOG.
BETTY BRANT. BEST OF BASSISTS. MY FORMER ROOMMATE. FULLY CHILL.

NO PLOTTING ESCAPE ON BAND TIME.
BUT CORN DOGS--
WE NEED TO FOCUS IF WE'RE GOING TO BE THE BEST.
YES, MA'AM.

THIS IS MY BAND. WE'RE CALLED THE MARY JANES. WE'RE GOOD.
WE USED TO BE BETTER. WE'LL BE BETTER AGAIN. WE JUST NEED TIME.
TIME HAS BEEN IN SORT OF SHORT SUPPLY LATELY.

BETTY? YOU NEED A RIDE?
THAT WOULD BE AWESOME.
AREN'T YOU GOING TO ASK ME?
DO YOU NEED A RIDE?
NO, I THINK I'M GOOD.

LET ME GUESS. YOU'RE GOING TO WALK.
SOMETHING LIKE THAT.
I'M MEETING HARRY FOR DINNER.
SEE YOU TOMORROW!

TIME MAKES EVERYTHING BETTER.
TIME IS GOING TO MAKE ME BETTER TOO.

GWEN STACY.
SUPER HERO.
WOO-HOO!
ME BEING SPIDER-WOMAN--SPIDER-GWEN--WHATEVER--HASN'T ALWAYS BEEN EASY, BUT I'M SO GLAD MY BAND KNOWS NOW.
SECRET IDENTITIES COMPLICATE EVERYTHING.
IN BOTH GOOD WAYS AND BAD ONES.

WHY DO I STILL CHECK FOR *WITNESSES* BEFORE I CHANGE COSTUMES?

HABIT, I GUESS. IT'S GOOD TO BE CAREFUL.

CAUTION KEEPS YOU BREATHING.

I LIKE BREATHING.

AFTER THE LAST FEW WEEKS...I HAVE A NEW APPRECIATION FOR IT.

PEOPLE SHOULD TRY TO BE ON TIME.
BAD THINGS CAN HAPPEN WHEN YOU'RE NOT.

THE ONLY BAD THINGS TONIGHT ARE HAPPENING TO OUR ARTERIES.
COME ON. I'LL BUY YOU A MILKSHAKE.
WHAT IS THIS, 1950?
A GOOD MILKSHAKE IS TIMELESS.

TIMELESS.
I LIKE THE SOUND OF THAT.

ARE YOU SURE YOU'RE OKAY?
I'M FINE.
PEOPLE ONLY SAY THAT WHEN THEY'RE NOT FINE.
I KNOW. I JUST...
I DON'T KNOW HOW TO EXPLAIN.
IT'S BIG AND IT'S WEIRD AND IT'S COMPLICATED.

I HAVE SOME EXPERIENCE WITH BIG, WEIRD AND COMPLICATED. AGENT OF S.H.I.E.L.D., REMEMBER?
I'M YOUR FRIEND. I WORRY ABOUT YOU.

OKAY, SO YOU KNOW THE OTHER NIGHT, WHEN I RAN OUT OF HERE?
YEAH?
THERE ARE THESE... BEINGS...CALLED THE INHERITORS--*
*FOR THE REST OF GWEN'S TERRIFYING TALE, SEE SPIDER-GEDDON!

HAVE YOU... THAT'S WHERE YOU WERE ALL LAST WEEK?
YEAH.
GOING TO FUNERALS.
MORE ARRANGING THEM, I GUESS.

THEIR FAMILIES WOULD NEVER HAVE KNOWN.
WITHOUT ME, THEIR FAMILIES WOULD...
THEY WOULD JUST NEVER HAVE KNOWN.

YOU'RE AMAZING.
...
I MEAN IT. THAT'S...DO YOU UNDERSTAND WHAT YOU'VE DONE, GWEN STACY?
FORGET FIGHTING VILLAINS AND SAVING THE WORLD. THAT'S WHAT IT MEANS TO BE A HERO.

THANK YOU? I THINK.

YOU'RE WELCOME. AND I'M GETTING YOU ANOTHER MILKSHAKE.
YOU DON'T HAVE TO--
HUSH! HEROES GET MILKSHAKES.
HAHAHA!
I DIDN'T DO IT FOR THE MILKSHAKE.

ALTHOUGH IT WAS A GOOD MILKSHAKE.
I DID IT BECAUSE SOMEONE HAD TO.
THERE WASN'T ANYBODY--*HUH?*
THAT'S NEW. AND DIFFERENT.
AND...BAD? MAYBE BAD.

PROBABLY NOT BAD. MY SPIDER-SENSE IS BEING CHILL.
WHY IS EVERYTHING *COMPLICATED?*
SPIDER-WOMAN!
...YEAH?
I'M SO GLAD I CAUGHT YOU! MY BROTHER LIVES IN THIS BUILDING. HE SAID HE'D SEEN YOU SWINGING BY A FEW TIMES.
I NEED YOUR HELP.
THIS IS NOT GETTING ANY LESS WEIRD.
IS IT NINJAS? BECAUSE I'M ***OUT*** OF THE NINJA BUSINESS.

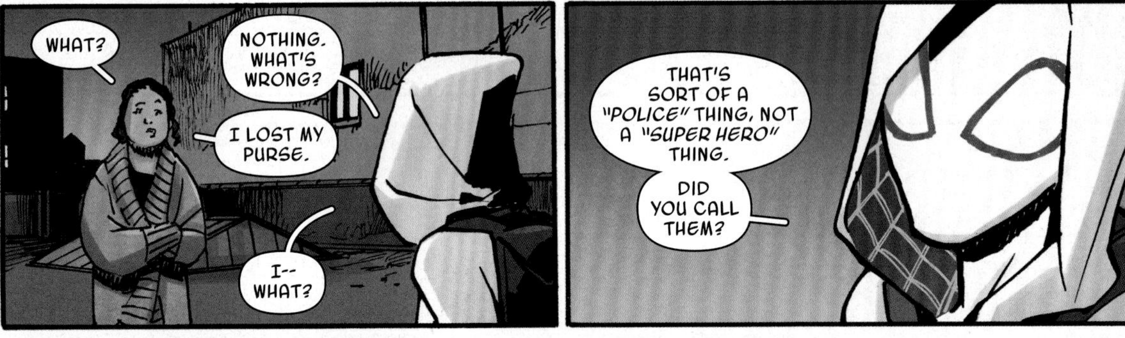
WHAT?
NOTHING. WHAT'S WRONG?
I LOST MY PURSE.
I-- WHAT?
THAT'S SORT OF A *"POLICE"* THING, NOT A *"SUPER HERO"* THING.
DID YOU CALL THEM?

I'M SORT OF ILLEGALLY SUBLETTING AN APARTMENT FROM A FRIEND.
I CAN'T CALL THE POLICE OR A LOCKSMITH WITHOUT GETTING US BOTH EVICTED.
I DON'T CARE ABOUT THE PURSE, I JUST NEED MY ***KEYS.***
DO YOU KNOW HOW HARD IT IS TO FIND AN AFFORDABLE PLACE IN A GOOD NEIGHBORHOOD?
TELL ME WHAT IT LOOKS LIKE AND WHERE YOU LOST IT.
I'LL KEEP AN EYE OUT.
I BET THIS NEVER HAPPENS TO SPIDER-MAN.

HOME
SWEET
HOME.

I SHOULD PROBABLY LOOK INTO GETTING MY OWN PLACE AGAIN, BUT IT'S NICE TO BE BACK.
DAD MISSED ME WHILE I WAS AWAY. AND I MISSED HIM.
DAD! I'M HOME!
IN THE KITCHEN!

HOW WAS REHEARSAL?
GOOD. LOUD. IS THAT SPAGHETTI?
I THOUGHT YOU WERE GETTING A BITE WITH HARRY.
I COULD EAT AGAIN.

MEANING YOU WEB-SLUNG YOUR WAY HOME.
IT'S CLEANER THAN THE SUBWAY.
IS IT SAFER?
I'VE SEEN MORE THAN MY FAIR SHARE OF MUGGERS, AND NONE OF THEM HAVE BEEN IN MIDAIR.

I GUESS THAT'S TRUE.
SET THE TABLE. DINNER'S READY.

THIS IS NICE.

THIS IS...MAYBE THIS IS WHAT THINGS WOULD HAVE BEEN LIKE IF I'D NEVER BEEN BITTEN.

JUST ME AND DAD AND DAD'S SPAGHETTI AND--

DAD? IS THERE ZUCCHINI IN THIS SAUCE?

DOCTOR'S ORDERS.

I'M SPIDER-WOMAN, AND I SAY THAT'S WEIRD.

GOOD THING I'M DOING THE COOKING FOR AS LONG AS I'M ON LEAVE.

YEAH. GOOD THING.

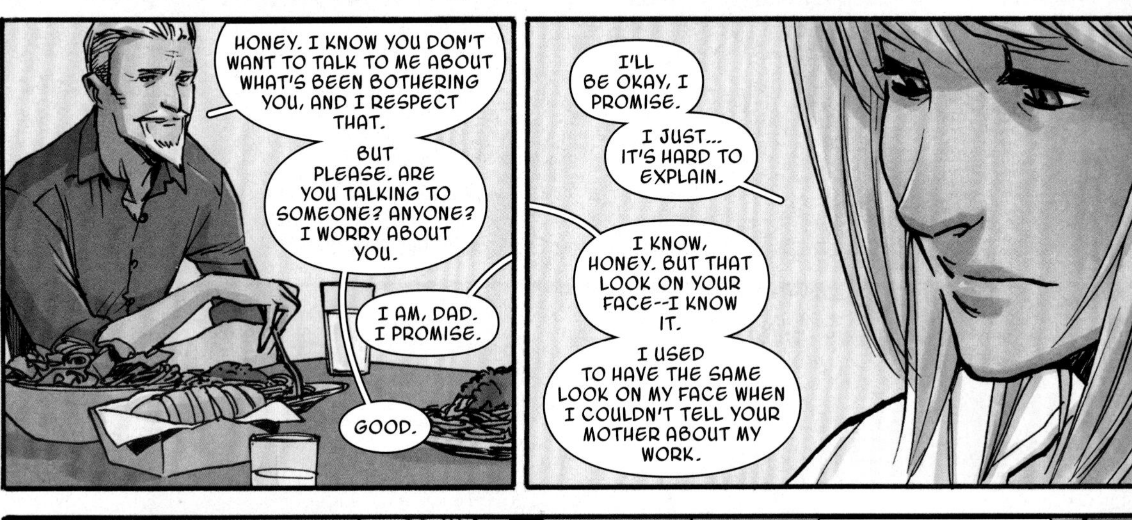

"--I'M GOING TO HAVE ONE."

I CAN DO THIS. JUST OPEN THE DOOR.

IT'S SIMPLE. EASY. I CAN DO THIS.

REGISTRAR'S OFFICE

I CAN'T DO THIS.

SPIDER-WOMAN CAN DO ANYTHING. WHEN I'M WEARING A MASK, I CAN FIGHT INHERITORS, I CAN BURY MY FRIENDS, I CAN DO ANYTHING.

I DON'T HAVE A MASK ON NOW. I CAN'T DO THIS.

WHY IS REAL LIFE SO SCARY?

EXCUSE ME?

ARE YOU **GWEN STACY?**

WHAT SHE MEANS IS, ARE YOU **SPIDER-WOMAN?**

UM. YEAH.

STUPID, STUPID, STUPID.

YOU BLEW YOUR *SECRET IDENTITY.*

YOU WENT TO *PRISON.* ON *PURPOSE.*

ALL YOU GET TO BE IS *SPECIAL*.
FOREVER.

LOOKS LIKE THEY DISABLED THE CAMERAS.
THEY PROBABLY HAVE AN INSIDE MAN. NOT GREAT.
AND THERE'S NO WAY TO GET THE CIVILIANS CLEAR.

WELL, HERE GOES.
YOU KNOW, I WAS HAVING A PRETTY LOUSY DAY.

YOU'RE NOT MAKING IT BETTER.
CLONK

THWP
NO GUN FOR YOU!

THHWP
WHAT DID I JUST SAY?!
HEH.
OKAY. LET'S GO.

OKAY. WELL.
I FEEL A LITTLE BIT BETTER NOW.

UM. HI.
SORRY ABOUT ALL THE, YOU KNOW, TERRIFYING ROBBERY STUFF.

YEAH!
...OH.

WELL, OKAY.
I GUESS THAT'S COOL.

THAT WAS NICE.
I MEAN, EVERYTHING'S STILL COMPLICATED AND WEIRD, BUT THAT WAS STILL NICE.
NOW, IF I CAN JUST FIND THAT PURSE...

THIS IS A TERRIBLE IDEA.
STILL WORTH TRYING.

NO WAY.

"NO WAY."

YOU'RE HERE!
YEAH. UH, HI. I FOUND THIS.
YOUR KEYS ARE INSIDE.
WALLET'S GONE, BUT...KEYS.

THANK YOU SO MUCH!
YOU'VE SAVED MY LIFE, REALLY.
IT WAS NO TROUBLE.
MY BROTHER LEFT ME SOME CASH, IN CASE YOU CAME BACK.

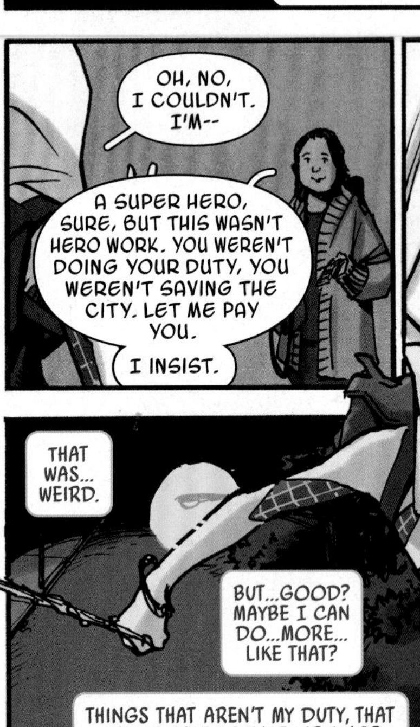
OH, NO, I COULDN'T. I'M--
A SUPER HERO, SURE, BUT THIS WASN'T HERO WORK. YOU WEREN'T DOING YOUR DUTY, YOU WEREN'T SAVING THE CITY. LET ME PAY YOU.
I INSIST.
PLEASE.
...I GUESS. THANKS.

THAT WAS... WEIRD.
BUT...GOOD? MAYBE I CAN DO...MORE... LIKE THAT?
THINGS THAT AREN'T MY DUTY, THAT PAY. IS THAT...IS THAT WRONG?
I COULD HELP DAD WITH THE RENT.
IF PEOPLE HAVE TO KNOW ME, I CAN USE IT.
MAYBE. AFTER I GET SOME RE--
ZZZZZZZZZZZZZZZZZZZ

ZZZZZZZZ

WE'D BEEN PLANNING THIS HEIST FOR WEEKS, AND SHE JUST... STROLLS IN.
SHE RUINED EVERYTHING.

SHE WAS SUPPOSED TO BE GONE.
THIS ISN'T GOING TO WORK.
WE NEED SPIDER-WOMAN OUT OF THE PICTURE.

SHE'S A LITTLE GIRL. BARELY MORE THAN A CHILD.
YOU REALLY WANT TO TELL ME THAT YOU CAN'T STOP A CHILD?

SHE HAS POWERS--
YOU WEREN'T THERE, SHE--
SHE'S A MENACE--
WE COULD RULE THIS CITY WITHOUT--
HER? WITHOUT HER?
ALL RIGHT, THEN.

LET'S GET RID OF SPIDER-WOMAN!

THEN.
I AM HERE TO TELL THE PEOPLE OF THIS CITY THAT WE WILL NOT BOW DOWN TO VIGILANTES. WE WILL NOT BE RULED BY FEAR.
WE ARE ALL THE FAMILY OF PETER PARKER TODAY, AND WE ARE STANDING TOGETHER TO SAY NO MORE.
THE SPIDER-WOMAN'S REIGN OF TERROR WILL END!

LIVE
THIS IS BULL.

CLCK

DADDY?
JAMESON'S ON ANOTHER "WE HAVE TO STOP THE SPIDER-WOMAN" KICK.
...AND YOU DON'T WANT HIM TO?
OF COURSE I DO.
OH.

BUT HE ACTS LIKE THE POLICE AREN'T EVEN TRYING. LIKE WE'RE USELESS.
BELIEVE ME, WHEN SPIDER-WOMAN IS BROUGHT TO JUSTICE, IT WON'T BE BY ANY MAYORAL TASK FORCE. IT'LL BE GOOD, OLD-FASHIONED LEGWORK.
HEH.

I MEAN, SPIDERS, LEGS...
I'LL JUST GO TO MY ROOM.
YOU DO THAT.

NOW.
--AND IN LIGHT OF HER RELEASE, I SAY THAT I AM PROUD TO WELCOME SPIDER-WOMAN HOME.
SHE IS A SYMBOL OF INTEGRITY AND STRENGTH THAT STANDS FOR THIS CITY, A SHINING REMINDER THAT HERE, WE PAY OUR DEBTS. HERE, WE--
UGH.
WOLVES. THEY'RE ALL WOLVES.
THEY FOLLOW THE STRONG AND ATTACK THE WEAK.
MAYOR JAMESON ISN'T THE WORST OF THEM, BUT I DON'T TRUST HIM.
THINK YOU CAN COPY THIS, BUT WITHOUT THE HOLE IN THE SLEEVE?
GWEN STACY. SPIDER-WOMAN. HARD ON CLOTHES.
YOU ARE SO COOL.
SYMBIOTE. BETTER THAN DRY CLEANING.
SUPER-HEROING HAS ITS UPS AND DOWNS.
BUT NEVER NEEDING TO DO LAUNDRY AGAIN?
DEFINITE BONUS.

GOOD MORNING, BEST FATHER IN THE WORLD!
NO, YOU CANNOT HAVE A PUPPY.
WHEN'S THE LAST TIME I ASKED FOR A PUPPY?
YOU WERE NINE. I HAVE A LONG MEMORY.
GEORGE STACY. POLICE CAPTAIN (ON LEAVE). FATHER (PERMANENT ASSIGNMENT).

I WANT A PONY NOW.
A ***SPIDER-***PONY. THAT CAN CLIMB WALLS AND HELP ME FIGHT CRIME.
IS THAT SO.
YOU'VE JUST INVENTED ***SLEIPNIR.***
WHAT?
READ A BOOK.

YOU'RE GOING IN TO TALK TO H.R. TODAY, RIGHT?
THAT'S MY TOAST. I WORKED HARD TO MAKE THAT.
ARE YOU SURE YOU'RE READY TO GO BACK TO WORK?
SINCE MY OWN DAUGHTER IS APPARENTLY A ***THIEF,*** I'M CLEARLY NEEDED.
TOAST THEFT IS NOT A FEDERAL OFFENSE.
IT'S TRAGIC.

WE'RE GETTING OFF TOPIC, WHICH IS YOUR BEST-NESS.
OF COURSE. TELL ME HOW BEST I AM.
FINEST OF FATHERS, BEST OF MEN.
WHAT DO YOU WANT?
DO I HAVE TO WANT SOMETHING?

OKAY! OKAY. STOP GIVING ME THE ***DAD FACE.***
I FOUND A WOMAN'S PURSE LAST NIGHT.
SHE ***PAID*** ME.
DO YOU WANT A COOKIE? YOU ALREADY HAVE MY TOAST.

ALL RIGHT, AND...?
AND SUPER HEROES DON'T USUALLY GET **PAID.**
YOU DON'T PAY THE **COPS** TO SOLVE A CRIME, YOU DON'T PAY A **SUPER HERO** FOR SAVING THE DAY.
WELL, TAXES EXIST, SO TECHNICALLY YOU **DO** PAY THE POLICE, BUT GO ON.

I WAS THINKING. I CAN'T EXACTLY GET A JOB, YOU KNOW?
HIGH SCHOOL DIPLOMA. NO DEGREE. PRISON RECORD.
BUT THIS, I CAN DO. ODD JOBS. **HELPING** PEOPLE. I CAN BE USEFUL **AND** PAY THE RENT.
I WANT TO KNOW THAT YOU'RE OKAY WITH THIS.
HONESTLY, I'M **NOT.**

WHAT?
I KNOW BEING **SPIDER-WOMAN** IS IMPORTANT TO YOU. IF I WERE GOING TO ASK YOU TO STOP, I WOULD HAVE DONE IT ALREADY.
I KNOW YOU FEEL LIKE YOU NEED TO USE YOUR POWERS TO **HELP** PEOPLE.
BUT YOU'RE **ALMOST** AN ADULT, SO THAT DOESN'T MEAN I HAVE TO BE HAPPY WITH IT.

LOOK. **EVERYONE** KNOWS I'M SPIDER-WOMAN. I CAN'T PUT THAT RABBIT BACK IN THE HAT.
AT LEAST THIS WAY, PEOPLE GET USED TO SEEING ME AROUND, IN COSTUME, NOT DOING ANY HARM.
IT'S LIKE COMMUNITY SERVICE, ONLY AT THE END, WE CAN KEEP BUYING FOOD.
MMM, FOOD. DELICIOUS, EXPENSIVE FOOD.

THIS ISN'T YOU ASKING FOR PERMISSION, IS IT?
NO. IT'S THE STEP BETWEEN THAT AND BEGGING FOR FORGIVENESS.
FINE. JUST PLEASE--

"--BE CAREFUL."

I'M *ALWAYS* CAREFUL.

SURE, SOMETIMES I'M CAREFULLY DODGING BULLETS, BUT I'M *CAREFUL*.

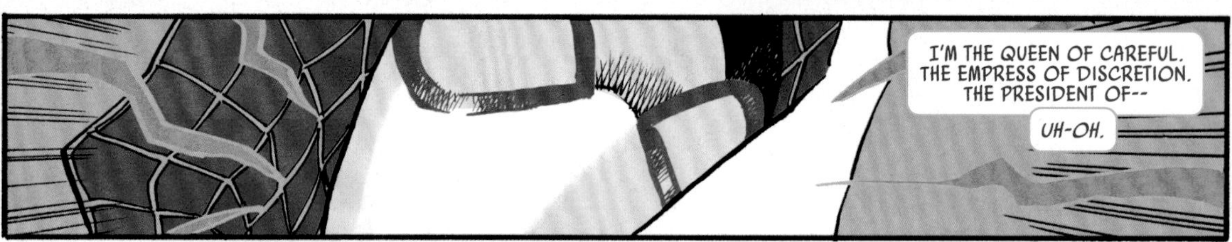

I THOUGHT WE TALKED ABOUT THIS WHEN I GAVE YOU **PINE CONE.**

HAMSTERS ARE NOT WELL-SUITED TO A LIFE OF **CRIME.**

SPIDER-WOMAN!

GOT IT IN ONE. NOW TELL THE NICE MAN YOU'RE SORRY, PUT DOWN THE GUN, AND WALK AWAY.

HOW HAVE YOU BEEN? SHOULD I STILL CALL YOU SPIDER-WOMAN, OR DO YOU PREFER **GWEN?**

UGH, SOMETIMES I MISS HAVING A SECRET IDENTITY.

AND IT'S SPIDER-WOMAN, PLEASE.

YOU **KNOW** EACH OTHER?

WE'VE MET.

I'M HER **ARCH-NEMESIS!**

YOU'RE REALLY, REALLY NOT.

I'M THE BODEGA BANDI--

THWIPP

AW, COME ON.

CAN I AT LEAST HAVE THE SUNFLOWER SEEDS?

LEAVE. NOW.

HERE. GIVE THIS TO THE POLICE WHEN THEY SHOW UP.
SORRY ABOUT ALL THIS.
THAT'S IT?
IT'S A CAP GUN.

NOT EVERYTHING HAS TO BE--
--AH. HARD.

JINGLE
ARE YOU ALL RIGHT?
JUST A HEADACHE. I'M FINE.
WELL, THAT WAS GREAT.
WHO GETS A HEADACHE IN THE MIDDLE OF FIGHTING CRIME?
CLOSED

I HOPE BETTY HAS ASPIRIN.
THIS BETTER BE A SLOW DAY.
ATM

BETTY BRANT. BANDMATE. BASSIST. BONKERS. DOESN'T OBJECT TO "SUPER HERO WEIRDNESS."
MUCH.
ALSO USUALLY HAS FOOD.
PIZZA

THUMP
HMM?
RRRRRRRRR?

WHAT THE-- GWEN!

WHAT ARE YOU DOING OUT THERE?
OH, JUST HANGING AROUND.
ICAN'TBELIEVEYOUJUSTSAIDTHAT.
SORRY. LONG DAY.

IT'S TEN THIRTY IN THE MORNING.
OKAY, LONG MORNING.
DO YOU HAVE ANY ASPIRIN? OR DONUTS? OR BOTH?
DOESN'T YOUR FATHER FEED YOU?
ONLY ON THE WEEKENDS.

TWO DONUTS LATER.
SO WE CAN SET YOU UP A BUSINESS PLAN, BUT YOU'RE GOING TO HAVE TO MAKE SOME DECISIONS.
LIKE HOW YOU'RE GOING TO DEAL WITH TAXES.
TAXES?
THIS ISN'T A LEMONADE STAND, GWEN.
DONUTS

IT COULD BE.
"SPIDER-WOMAN'S ODD JOBS AND LEMONADE."
I'VE HAD YOUR COOKING. PASS.

LOOK, ARE YOU SURE ABOUT THIS?
THERE'S A LOT MORE INVOLVED WITH RUNNING A SMALL BUSINESS THAN HAVING A WEBSITE.
AND SUPER-POWERS.
THAT PART'S UNUSUAL, I'LL ADMIT.

I CAN HELP PEOPLE. IT'S WHAT I'M GOOD AT.
CAN'T GO TO COLLEGE, CAN'T GET A REAL JOB, BUT I CAN HELP PEOPLE.
THEY JUST NEED TO KNOW HOW TO FIND ME.
IN THAT CASE...

...WE'RE LIVE.
WE ARE?
WE ARE.
PEOPLE CAN FIND THIS? CAN FIND ME?
IF THEY UNDERSTAND HOW THE INTERNET WORKS, YEAH.

OMIGOSH.
THANK YOU SO MUCH!
THANK ME WHEN YOU GET MY BILL.
MRRRRROWL.

YOU'RE DOING **WHAT?!**

I'M ADVERTISING MY SERVICES AS SPIDER-WOMAN.

WITH **WHAT** FREE TIME?

YOU CAN'T BE SUPER-HEROING AND REHEARSING AND WORKING FOR THE WHOLE CITY.

IF YOU'RE GONNA BE HERE, WE NEED YOU TO **BE HERE,** GWEN.

MARY JANE WATSON. LEADER OF THE BAND. VOCALIST. YELLS REALLY LOUD.

GLORY GRANT. PLAYS THE KEYS. NOT CURRENTLY TALKING MJ DOWN.

SORRY ABOUT, YOU KNOW, BEFORE. YOU WERE A GOOD ROOMMATE, IT'S JUST--
IT'S OKAY. I GET IT.
GOOD REHEARSAL TONIGHT. WE'RE STARTING TO GEL AGAIN.
YOU KNOW, I THINK WE ARE.

I REALLY DON'T MIND.
LIVING WITH A SUPER HERO IS DANGEROUS.
I JUST NEED TO KEEP EVERYONE AS SAFE AS I CAN.

THE MORE PEOPLE THINK OF ME AS A NORMAL PART OF LIFE--
--THEIR FRIENDLY NEIGHBORHOOD SPIDER-WOMAN--
--THE SAFER EVERYONE I CARE ABOUT WILL BE.

I CAN DO THIS.

I CAN.
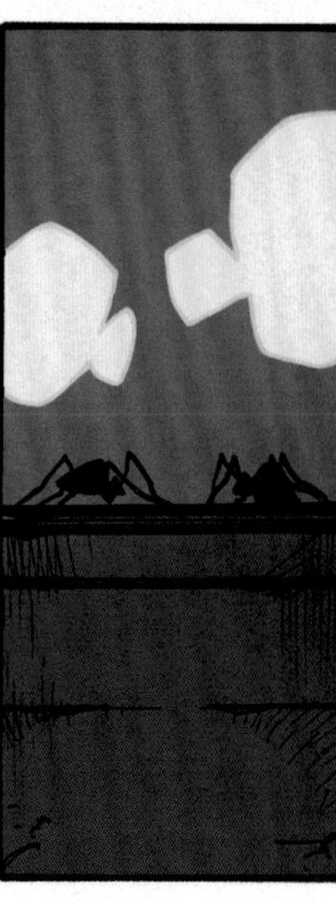

NO MESSAGES YET.
BING!
MY FIRST MESSAGE! IT'S REALLY HAPPEN--
WHAT? EW, NO. THIS ISN'T A DATING APP.
NO MESSAGES YET.
(WE'RE PRETENDING THAT DIDN'T HAPPEN.)

UGH. UGH. WHY DOES EVERYTHING HAVE TO BE SO HARD?
I JUST WANT TO SAVE THE CITY, HELP PEOPLE AND PLAY THE DRUMS.
IT'S NOT LIKE I WANT TO BE A UNICORN ASTRONAUT SPACE PRINCESS.
I HAVEN'T SINCE I WAS FIVE.

WEBSITES AND FLIERS AND EVERYTHING IS DIFFICULT.
CRIME IS EASIER. CRIME JUST HAPPENS.

THWAP
TROUBLE? FIND ME! SPIDER WOMAN
ALSO, YOU CAN PUNCH CRIME.

CAN YOU PUNCH WAITING? NO, YOU CANNOT.
ONLY FIVE HUNDRED FLIERS TO GO AND PLEASE, PLEASE, PLEASE LET ME FIND A MUGGER.

AHHHHHHHH!
RIGHT ON SCHEDULE.

I DON'T *SEE* ANYONE...

YOU MADE SOME BAD DECISIONS, LITTLE SPIDER.
LITTLE SPIDERS GET SQUASHED.

WHAM

FIVE ON ONE? SERIOUSLY?

WHAT THE @#G@# WAS THIS?
SOME KIND OF INITIATION RITUAL?

THERE'S A BAD MOON RISING, YOU LITTLE BRAT.
YOU'RE GOING TO PAY.
UGH. CLICHÉ MUCH?

WHAT THE--?

CAN'T--

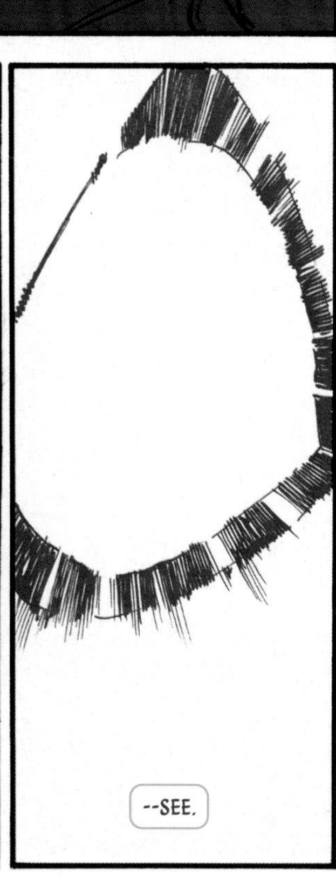
--SEE.

HOW...?

WHAT...?

I DON'T... HOW DID I... WHERE *AM* I?

OH!

EXCELLENT. THIS IS EXACTLY WHAT WE NEEDED.
THEN I SUGGEST A PAIR OF **PLIERS.**
I THINK THAT LITTLE FREAK CRACKED ONE OF MY TEETH.

EASY FOR YOU TO SAY. YOU DIDN'T GET PUNCHED.
KICKED.
KICKED **AND** PUNCHED.

I ASSURE YOU, I'M DOING MY PART.
SOON, WE'LL KNOW EXACTLY HOW TO TAKE DOWN **SPIDER-WOMAN.**
"WE." WHAT AN INTERESTING CHOICE OF WORDS.

I...I JUST MEANT...
IT'S A FUNNY NAME YOU CHOSE FOR YOURSELF. "JACKAL." THEY'RE SCAVENGERS, YOU KNOW. WEAK.

LITTLE BETTER THAN PREY, IF YOU ASK ME.
I HAVE THE FOOTAGE YOU WANTED.

SEE? SHE HITS HARD, BUT SHE COUNTS ON HITTING HARD.
NO TECHNIQUE. JUST BLUNT FORCE.
IS THAT ALL?
LOOK AT THIS.

SHE'S TAKING ON CLIENTS.
TROUBLE? FIND ME! SPIDERWOMAN
THAT'S ADORABLE.
ARE YOU PLANNING TO HIRE HER?

WE KNOW SHE'S CAPTAIN STACY'S DAUGHTER, AND WE KNOW WE CAN'T ATTACK HER AT HOME.
THE POLICE DON'T LIKE HER, BUT THEY'LL DEFEND HIM.
THIS, THOUGH... SHE'S STRETCHING HERSELF THIN.
SOMETHING'S GOT TO GIVE.

HMPH.

KEEP AN EYE ON HER.
THROW HER SOME WORK. A FEW CATS IN TREES.
WE CAN GIVE HER A FEW DAYS TO FAIL.

GOOD NIGHT, GWEN.
GOOD NIGHT, HARRY.

HEADACHES ARE NORMAL. DINNER IS NORMAL.
I COULD GET USED TO A LITTLE NORMAL.
I WONDER IF NORMAL CAN GET USED TO ME.

WELL, THIS IS HAPPENING.
IF I WERE MAKING A LIST OF EVERYTHING THAT'S HAPPENING RIGHT NOW, IT WOULD JUST SAY "THIS."
THE CAPITOL
THIS IS MY LIFE. THIS IS MY FIGHT. THIS IS MY...DATE NIGHT?
FIGHTING CRIME IS SO MUCH EASIER.
HERE WE GO.
GWEN!
THIS IS HAPPENING.
WOW.
WOW.
GWEN STACY, A.K.A. SPIDER-WOMAN. SUPER HERO. DOESN'T WEAR HIGH HEELS.

HA!

SMOOTH, STACY.

REAL SMOOTH.

THIS IS...THIS IS FANCY.
NICE RESTAURANTS ARE OFTEN FANCY.
IS THE FOOD FREE? I ASK BECAUSE THERE ARE NO PRICES ON MY MENU.
THE FOOD IS SORT OF THE OPPOSITE OF FREE.
I'D BE HAPPY WITH A CORN DOG.
THEY HAVE CORN DOGS HERE.
REALLY.
YES!
...TECHNICALLY.

"TECHNICALLY"?

HOW IS SOMETHING "TECHNICALLY" A CORN DOG?
WHEN IT'S BRAISED PORK SHANK SERVED ON A BED OF POLENTA.
...
THAT IS NOT A CORN DOG.

IT'S LIKE A CORN DOG.
IT'S REALLY, REALLY NOT.
TRY IT. MAYBE YOU'LL LIKE IT.
MR. OSBORN?

YES?
WHILE WE APPRECIATE YOUR PATRONAGE, YOU MIGHT FIND ANOTHER ESTABLISHMENT MORE TO YOUR LIKING THIS EVENING.
WHAT?
I'M AFRAID I MUST REQUEST THAT YOU LEAVE.

WHY IN THE WORLD--
IT'S BECAUSE OF ME.

ISN'T IT?
YOU'RE NOT COMFORTABLE HAVING ME HERE.
IS IT BECAUSE I'M A CRIMINAL? OR BECAUSE I'M A **SUPER HERO?**
WE WOULD PREFER TO **AVOID** THAT WORD.
WHICH ONE? "CRIMINAL"?
BECAUSE I PROMISE YOU, I'M NOT THE ONLY ONE.
HOW MUCH WHITE-COLLAR CRIME DO YOU THINK YOUR CLIENTELE COMMITS?

I'M NOT ALL RIGHT. I DON'T EVEN KNOW WHAT "ALL RIGHT" IS ANYMORE.
IS IT SAVING THE CITY? BECAUSE I DID THAT, AND THEY HATED ME.
IS IT MAKING AMENDS? BECAUSE I DID THAT TOO, AND THEY **STILL** HATED ME.
IS IT BURYING MY FRIENDS? BECAUSE I'VE BURIED SO MANY-- SO MANY OF THE PEOPLE I LOVED.

AND WHEN I BURIED PETER, THEY HATED ME FOR THAT TOO.
I DON'T BELONG HERE. I CAN'T...
I CHOSE THIS WORLD. OUT OF AN ENTIRE MULTIVERSE. I CHOSE **MY** WORLD. WHEN DOES **IT** START CHOOSING **ME?**

BUT, GWEN...**I** CHOOSE YOU.

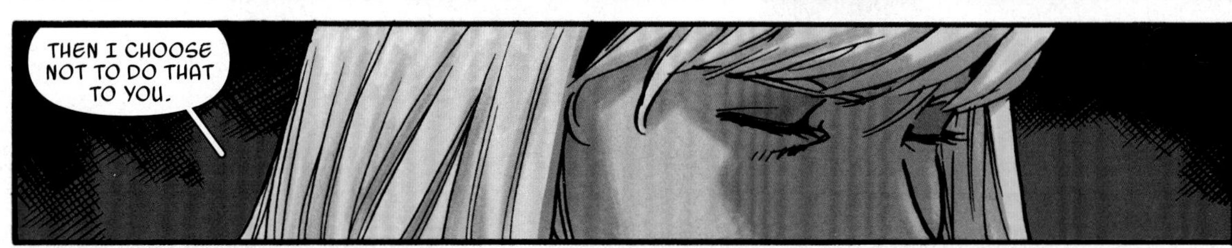
THEN I CHOOSE NOT TO DO THAT TO YOU.

GWEN...

HE CAPITOL
GWEN!!!
I CAN'T DO THIS. I DON'T GET TO DO THIS.
I CHOSE TO BE A HERO. I LET THEM CALL ME A VILLAIN.
UNTIL I FIND A WAY TO BALANCE THOSE TWO THINGS, MY LIFE...
...MY LIFE DOESN'T GET TO BE THIS EASY.

CRIME MAKES SENSE.

FIGHTING CRIME MAKES MORE SENSE.

I WAS NEVER A JOCK IN HIGH SCHOOL, BUT I'M STARTING TO GET THEM.

WHEN YOU'RE MOVING, WHEN YOU'RE TRUSTING YOUR BODY...

I DON'T HAVE TO THINK. I JUST HAVE TO DO.

AHHHHHH!

I DON'T HAVE TO WONDER IF THEY HATE ME.

I'M HITTING THEM. OF *COURSE* THEY HATE ME.

I WAS STUPID TO THINK MY NORMAL LIFE WOULD BE WAITING FOR ME.
THERE'S NO NORMAL FOR ME. NOT ANYMORE. I SHOULD JUST--
BZZZZZ
HUH?

NO WAY.
NO WAY.
NO WAY!

WHEN BETTY SET UP MY WEBSITE, I WAS HOPING, BUT--

I DIDN'T THINK ANYONE WOULD EVER--
I MEAN, IT'S BEEN A WEEK AND--
OH WOW OH WOW OH WOW

OKAY. BE COOL NOW. BE PROFESSIONAL.

BZZZZZZ

WHO IS IT?
SPIDER-WOMAN, HERE FOR LUIS.
...
SPIDER-GWEN?
SPIDER-WOMAN. BUT YES.
I NEED A NEW CODENAME.
YOU SENT ME AN EMAIL? ABOUT THE SCIENCE GIG?

IT'S ACTUALLY YOU?
DID YOU THINK YOU WERE EMAILING A REALLY AMBITIOUS COSPLAYER?
OH MY GOD!
BECAUSE SOME OF THEM ARE AMAZING, BUT THEY CAN'T STICK TO WALLS.
I'LL BE RIGHT DOWN.

OH MY GOD, YOU'RE REALLY YOU!
I THOUGHT WE'D ESTABLISHED THAT. HI, I'M SPIDER-WOMAN, AND YOU EMAILED ME. HOW CAN I HELP?
I THOUGHT YOU'D BE BOOKED OUT FOR, LIKE, YEARS.
WHAT CAN I SAY? I HAD AN OPENING.
NOW, WHAT CAN I DO FOR YOU?

WELL...
I NEED TO GET SOME AIR QUALITY SAMPLES. SOME ELEVATED AIR QUALITY SAMPLES...

MONDAY.

COLLECTING AIR QUALITY SAMPLES. OKAY, WEIRD, BUT NOT UNREASONABLE.

MAKING 200 BUCKS TO DO IT? ***AWESOME.*** MAYBE LETTING PEOPLE HIRE ME WILL WORK OUT AFTER ALL.

FRIDAY.
I'M GLAD YOU CALLED.
I'M GLAD YOU ANSWERED.

BETTY MANAGED TO GET THE MARY JANES A GIG, AND MJ IS **FREAKING** OUT.
SHE THINKS THIS IS GOING TO BE OUR BIG COMEBACK.
JUST TELL ME WHEN AND WHERE AND I'LL BE IN THE FRONT ROW.

YOU KNOW, I BELIEVE YOU WILL BE.
I DON'T REALLY HAVE A CHOICE HERE.
SOMEONE NEEDS TO REMIND YOU THAT YOU ONLY HAVE ONE PROM DATE, AND THAT'S ME.

YOU'RE NOT ONE OF THOSE GUYS WHO NEVER LETS GO OF HIGH SCHOOL, ARE YOU? BECAUSE I GOTTA TELL YOU, THAT'S WEIRD.
NO, I'M NOT ONE OF THOSE GUYS. I'M JUST SAYING, I ALREADY GOT THERE. I HAVE DIBS.
THERE ARE NO DIBS.
SPOKEN LIKE SOMEONE WITHOUT DIBS.

ARE YOU STILL HAVING HEADACHES?
...NO.
ARE YOU LYING?
MAYBE.
I DON'T LIKE THAT.

THE LYING OR THE HEADACHES?
HAVE YOU SEEN A DOCTOR?
I TOLD YOU, I'M FINE.
GWEN--

HARRY.
I WORRY.
I KNOW. BUT I CAN TAKE CARE--
BZZZZ
...OH NO. I HAVE TO GO.
ANOTHER SELFIE REQUEST?
NO--

"THERE'S BEEN AN ACCIDENT."

CAN'T JUST JUMP INTO THE FRAY. I'M TOUGH, BUT I CAN BURN.

NEED TO DO THIS SMART.

NEED TO FOCUS. DO THIS SO NO ONE GETS HURT. NEED TO--

ONE WAY

HEY, KIDDO.
YOU OKAY IN THERE?

OKAY. I UNDERSTAND.
I'M GOING TO GET YOU OUT OF HERE, OKAY?
CAN YOU UNLOCK THE DOOR FOR ME?

I KNOW YOU'RE PROBABLY NOT SUPPOSED TO TALK TO STRANGERS. I'M NOT A STRANGER.
I'M SPIDER-WOMAN. I'M A SUPER HERO, AND I NEED YOU TO UNLOCK THE DOOR.
I BET YOU'RE REALLY SCARED. I WOULD BE. LET'S GO FIND YOUR MOM.
U-LIFT

CLICK
GOOD GIRL.

WHAT'S YOUR NAME?
EISLEY.
IT'S NICE TO MEET YOU, EISLEY.

IT'S OKAY.
YOU'RE SAFE WITH ME.

THERE YOU GO. DON'T BE SCARED, OKAY?
I'M GOING TO GET YOU OUT OF HERE.

HELP ME... PLEASE.
OH NO.

I NEED YOU TO BE VERY BRAVE AND WAIT HERE FOR ME. CAN YOU DO THAT?
GOOD GIRL.
HOLD ON TIGHT, NOW.
AND CLOSE YOUR EYES FOR ME, OKAY? BE BRAVE.

HELLO?
WHERE ARE YOU?
DOWN... HERE.
IT'S GOING TO BE ALL RIGHT.
HOW? THERE'S A CAR ON MY BACK.
CAN YOU FEEL YOUR LEGS?
I CAN. MY NECK TOO.
OKAY. I DON'T REMEMBER MUCH FROM ***GREY'S ANATOMY,*** BUT I KNOW WE HAVE TO MOVE YOU CAREFULLY.
ARE YOU BLEEDING?
DON'T THINK SO. CAN SMELL... GAS...THOUGH.
TAKE A DEEP BREATH, AND TRY NOT TO MOVE.

SO I KNOW I, *UH,* JUST WEBBED YOUR ARMS.

BUT TRY TO HOLD ON, OKAY?

FSSSST

UH-OH.

UH-OH.

THIS IS GOING TO BE A LITTLE FAST!

PLEASE DON'T PUKE ON ME!

EISLEY, HANG ON-- WE'RE COMIN' TO YOU!

BOOM

THIS MAN IS HURT. I COULDN'T STOP THE FIRE.
SORRY.

WE KNEW IT WAS COMING. THANK YOU.
WE DIDN'T DISCUSS PAYMENT--
THANK YOU.

OH, NO! I DON'T GET PAID FOR BEING A SUPER HERO. JUST FOR, YOU KNOW, CATS IN TREES AND STUFF.
YOU'RE SURE?
I'M SUPER SURE.

WELL, THANK YOU.
DON'T WORRY ABOUT IT.

I'M JUST GLAD THAT I COULD HELP!

MY HEAD IS STILL KILLING ME.
I NEED TO KNOW WHAT THAT'S ABOUT, LIKE, YESTERDAY.
BUT WHO'S A BIG ENOUGH SCIENCE NERD TO HELP ME?
REED RICHARDS IS STILL IN SIXTH GRADE OR WHATEVER.
CINDY MOON IS IN JAIL, AND SHE DOESN'T EVEN KNOW HOW MY CURRENT POWERS WORK.
...NO, THERE'S ONLY ONE PERSON WHO KNOWS THAT. CRUD.
UGH, WHY IS MY LIFE SO COMPLICATED?
(AND I'M HUNGRY. AGAIN.)
HELLO, HARRY?
I NEED A FAVOR.
I NEED HELP GETTING INTO OSCORP.
I NEED TO TALK TO DR. ELSA BROCK.

THE
MARY
MARY JANES
THE
B.

OSCORP.
EARTH-65.

HARRY OSBORN. HIS DAD OWNS THE JOINT.

RING RING
COME ON, GWEN. PICK UP.

GWEN CAN'T COME TO THE PHONE RIGHT NOW. SHE'S DOING SOMETHING REALLY IMPORTANT WITH HER REALLY GOOD FRIEND.
WHO SHE KNOWS FORGIVES HER FOR RUINING THEIR DATE.
SHE ALSO KNOWS SHE'S A WEIRDO.
GWEN STACY. SPIDER-WOMAN. VERY LITTLE REGARD FOR GRAVITY.

YOU'RE NOT MAD AT ME, ARE YOU?
NO.
BECAUSE I KNOW YOU'RE A WEIRDO.
HEH.

I'M SORRY I'M LATE. I HAD TO STOP A ROBBERY.
HOW'S YOUR HEAD?
NOT GREAT. THEN AGAIN, IT'S USUALLY NOT GREAT THESE DAYS.
YOU REALLY THINK IT'S CONNECTED TO YOUR POWERS?
I RECOVER FROM INJURIES SO FAST IT'S EMBARRASSING. I HAVEN'T HAD A COLD OR FOOD POISONING IN YEARS.
AND I'VE SEEN THE WAY YOU EAT.
WHAT'S THAT SUPPOSED TO MEAN?
NO ONE EATS AS MANY CONVENIENCE STORE CORN DOGS AS YOU DO WITHOUT PAYING THE PRICE.
SUPER-POWERS ARE THE ONLY THING SAVING YOU FROM A LIFE OF SUFFERING AND ANTACIDS.
STOP THAT.
JUST BEING A GOOD FRIEND AND DISTRACTING YOU. DID IT WORK?
...A LITTLE.
THE HEADACHES ARE GETTING WORSE. MY POWERS SHOULD BE PREVENTING THEM.
THAT'S WHY I'M CONCERNED THAT SOMETHING'S WRONG WITH MY SYMBIOTE.
CAN'T YOU JUST, YOU KNOW, ASK IT? I THOUGHT IT WAS ALIVE.
IT IS, BUT WE CAN'T CHAT LIKE THAT. IT'S MORE COMPLICATED.

DR. BROCK CREATED THE SYMBIOTE. SHE SHOULD BE ABLE TO TELL ME IF IT'S SICK.
JUST THE HEADACHES.
IT'S STILL JUST HEADACHES, RIGHT? NOTHING ELSE IS GOING ON?
JUST THE HEADACHES, AND THE GUMMY SPIDERS.
THEY'RE EVERYWHERE WHEN I WAKE UP.
THEY'RE DOING THINGS I DIDN'T ASK THEM TO DO.

WHAT DO YOU MEAN, "SHE'S NOT HERE"?
I MEAN THERE IS NO ONE BY THAT NAME EMPLOYED AT OSCORP.
MAYBE YOU MISSPELLED IT.
SIR, IT'S A SIMPLE NAME. B-R-O-C-K. I SPELLED IT CORRECTLY.
LOOK AGAIN. WE HAVE AN APPOINTMENT.
I DON'T KNOW WHO YOUR APPOINTMENT IS WITH, BUT IT'S NOT WITH DR. ELSA BROCK.

WAIT, BUT--
TRY AGAIN.
=SIGH= YES, MR. OSBORN.

DR. ELSA BROCK IS NOT IN OUR SYSTEM. IS THERE SOMETHING ELSE I CAN DO FOR YOU?
YOU CAN CALL MY--
CAN I GET MY VISITOR'S PASS ANYWAY? I'M HERE WITH HARRY OSBORN. THAT'S GOOD ENOUGH, RIGHT?

RIGHT?

I LOVE MUSIC. I'VE ALWAYS LOVED MUSIC.
EVER TRY TO KEEP THE BEAT WITH A MIGRAINE?
THIS MAY BE THE MOST HEROIC THING I'VE EVER DONE.
WHICH IS SORT OF PATHETIC WHEN I PUT IT LIKE THAT.

DON'T THINK ABOUT HOW MUCH IT--
AHHHHHH!

GET IT OFF GET IT OFF GET IT OFF!
?!
Mary Janes

YOU DID THAT ON **PURPOSE,** DIDN'T YOU?

WANT TO TELL ME WHAT WE'RE DOING NOW?
WE'RE **SLEUTHING.**
YOU KNOW DR. BROCK WORKS HERE. **I** KNOW DR. BROCK WORKS HERE. WHY DOESN'T **THE COMPUTER** KNOW?
ALL RIGHT, VICTORIA MARS, CHILL.
GUEST
I AM ALWAYS CHILL. I'M SO CHILL I SHOULD HAVE SNOW POWERS.
DO SPIDERS LIKE THE SNOW?
NOT REALLY.
...YOU KNOW, IT'S SORT OF WEIRD THAT I DON'T HAVE MORE ICE-THEMED VILLAINS.
HA!
MAYBE WE SHOULDN'T GIVE THE UNIVERSE IDEAS, YOU KNOW? I MEAN-- GWEN? WHAT'S WRONG?
THIS IS SUPPOSED TO BE HER OFFICE.

SHE'S GONE.
SHE'S GONE, AND THERE'S SOMETHING **WRONG,** AND I DON'T KNOW WHAT TO DO.
CINDY MOON AND MATT MURDOCK ARE BOTH IN JAIL. I COULDN'T GO TO THEM IF I WANTED TO.
THERE'S NO ONE HERE TO **HELP** ME.
I CAN HELP YOU.
REALLY? HOW?

SO WHAT DO WE DO?

LIKE YOU SAID, WE VICTORIA MARS IT. WE FIND ELSA BROCK--

FIVE MINUTES AGO. I PHONED YOU TWICE.

SORRY. I WAS--

DISTRACTED? YOU DON'T GET TO BE DISTRACTED.

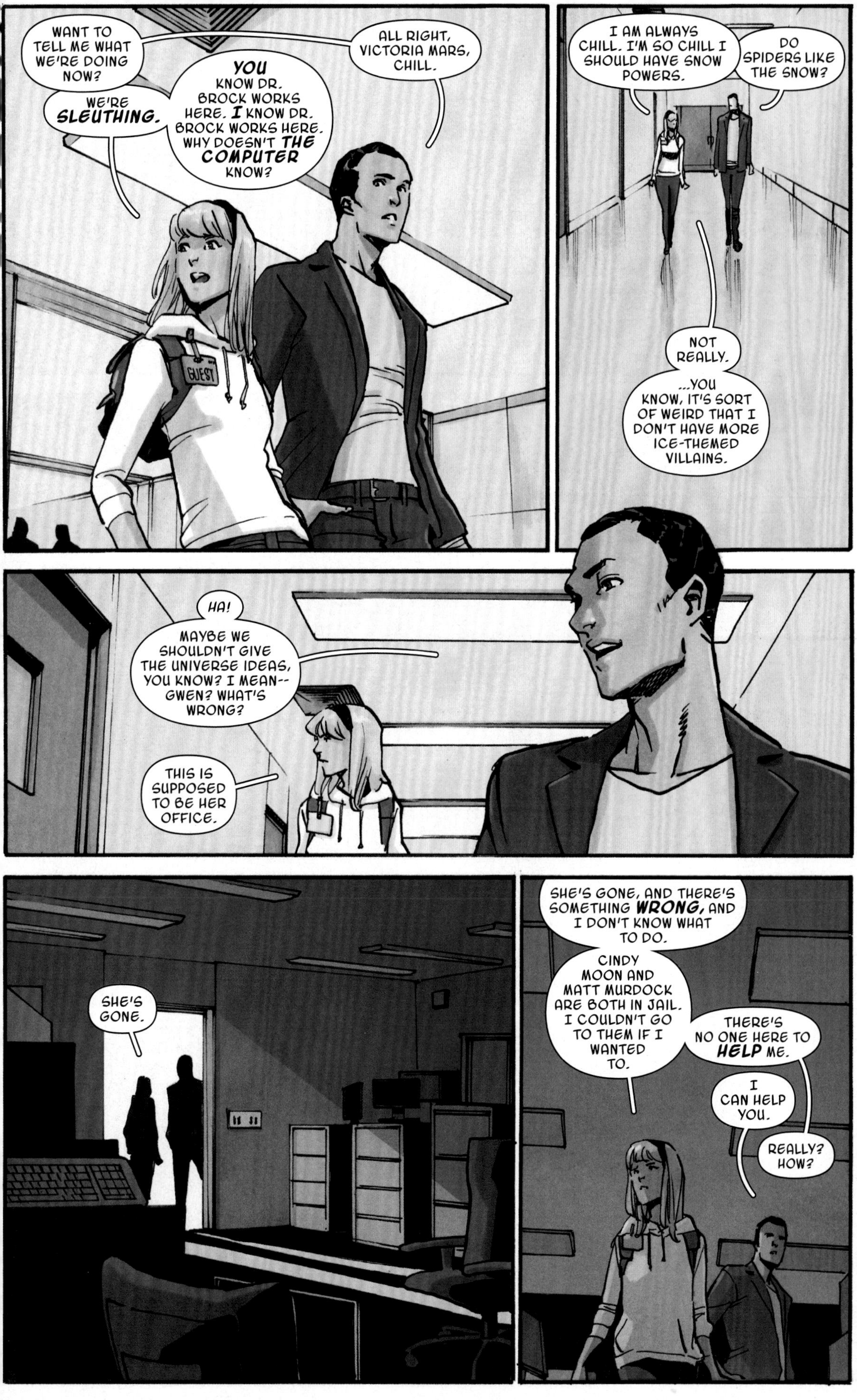

WANT TO TELL ME WHAT WE'RE DOING NOW?
ALL RIGHT, VICTORIA MARS, CHILL.
WE'RE **SLEUTHING.**
YOU KNOW DR. BROCK WORKS HERE. **I** KNOW DR. BROCK WORKS HERE. WHY DOESN'T **THE COMPUTER** KNOW?
GUEST

I AM ALWAYS CHILL. I'M SO CHILL I SHOULD HAVE SNOW POWERS.
DO SPIDERS LIKE THE SNOW?
NOT REALLY.
...YOU KNOW, IT'S SORT OF WEIRD THAT I DON'T HAVE MORE ICE-THEMED VILLAINS.

HA!
MAYBE WE SHOULDN'T GIVE THE UNIVERSE IDEAS, YOU KNOW? I MEAN-- GWEN? WHAT'S WRONG?
THIS IS SUPPOSED TO BE HER OFFICE.

HUH.

RIGHT. NO POWERS, NO POINT.
HARRY, I'M SORRY.
REALLY? BECAUSE YOU SOUNDED LIKE YOU MEANT IT JUST THERE.

I DIDN'T MEAN...YOU DON'T UNDERSTAND HOW MUCH YOU HELP ME. I SOMETIMES THINK YOU AND THE BAND ARE THE ONLY REASONS I STAY SANE.
I'M STILL GWEN TO YOU. FIRST, LAST AND ALWAYS. UPGRADED AND AWESOME, BUT GWEN.
THAT'S SO RARE NOWADAYS. I NEED YOU. NEVER THINK I DON'T NEED YOU.

SO WHAT DO WE DO?
LIKE YOU SAID, WE VICTORIA MARS IT. WE FIND ELSA BROCK--

"--NO MATTER WHERE SHE'S HIDING."
Zoogle
Dr. Elsa Brock
UH, EARTH TO GWEN STACY MUCH?

OH, SORRY.
ARE WE GETTING STARTED?
GREAT. NOW I GET TO ADD MJ MURDERING ME TO MY LIST OF PROBLEMS.

FIVE MINUTES AGO. I PHONED YOU TWICE.
SORRY. I WAS--
DISTRACTED? YOU DON'T GET TO BE DISTRACTED.
THE MARY JANES. ONLY THE COOLEST BAND IN THE MULTIVERSE.

THIS IS OUR BIG COMEBACK, GOT IT? THIS IS OUR CHANCE.
YOU DON'T GET TO BLOW THIS FOR US. NO DISAPPEARING. NO SUPER HERO BUSINESS MAKING YOU LATE.
THIS TIME-- THIS ONE TIME-- EVERYTHING IS GOING TO BE PERFECT. UNDERSTAND?
YES.
I DIDN'T HEAR YOU.
YES, MJ.

GREAT. NOW LET'S ROCK.
ON IT.

DON'T LET HER GET TO YOU. SHE'S JUST ANXIOUS.
I FIGHT ACTUAL SUPER VILLAINS.
SO YOU'RE SAYING MJ DOESN'T SCARE YOU ANYMORE?
UH, MJ TERRIFIES ME.
I HEARD THAT!

I LOVE MUSIC. I'VE ALWAYS LOVED MUSIC.
EVER TRY TO KEEP THE BEAT WITH A MIGRAINE?
THIS MAY BE THE MOST HEROIC THING I'VE EVER DONE.
WHICH IS SORT OF PATHETIC WHEN I PUT IT LIKE THAT.
Mary Janes
JUST KEEP MOVING, KEEP THE BEAT GOING, DON'T THINK TOO HARD.
DON'T THINK ABOUT HOW MUCH IT--
AHHHHHH!
GET IT OFF GET IT OFF GET IT OFF!
?!
Mary Janes
YOU DID THAT ON PURPOSE, DIDN'T YOU?
WHAT?

MY TURN.

AHHHHH--
WHAM

RUN! RUN!
GOING SOMEWHERE?
THWIP

KRAK

NOW.
WHO'S READY FOR A CIVICS LESSON?

STILL.
A CALORIE MIGHT HELP.
SWINGING THROUGH THE CITY IS ALWAYS GREAT, HEADACHE OR NO HEADACHE.
THIS IS THE PART THAT MAKES UP FOR SO MUCH OF THE REST.
RIGHT ON SCHEDULE.
A REAL LIVE SUPER HERO?
WHOOPS. GUESS NOT.
JUST REMEMBER, YOU STARTED IT.

CALORIES. CALORIES ARE GOOD.
CALORIES MAKE MY HEAD HURT LESS.
MJ SHOULD EAT A CALORIE.

MJ SHOULD--I DON'T KNOW WHAT MJ SHOULD DO. BREATHE, I GUESS.
I SHOULDN'T BE MAD AT HER FOR DOING WHAT I SAY I WANT. SHE STILL TREATS ME LIKE GWEN INSTEAD OF SPIDER-WOMAN.

NOW I JUST NEED SOMETHING TO HIT.

COME ON. WE'RE ON A SCHEDULE HERE.
YEAH, YEAH.
REALLY?

BUT IF YOU'D HURRIED, YOU WOULD NEVER HAVE MET ME.
AREN'T I WORTH THE WAIT?

IT WAS ONE OF YOUR **SPIDERS!**
YOU DON'T CARE ABOUT THIS SHOW. YOU BARELY CARE ABOUT THIS **BAND.**
I--I DIDN'T--
IS IT BECAUSE YOU'RE NOT THE FRONT WOMAN? CAN'T STAND NOT BEING IN THE SPOTLIGHT?

OKAY, MJ, YOU NEED TO COOL DOWN. GWEN DIDN'T DO ANYTHING ON PURPOSE.
GWEN, MAYBE NOW WOULD BE A GOOD TIME FOR YOU TO TAKE A WALK.
SERIOUSLY?
UNLESS YOU FEEL LIKE DEATH BY GUITARIST?

GOT IT. SEE YOU ALL TOMORROW.
NOT IF I SEE YOU FIRST!
HONEY, THAT DIDN'T EVEN MAKE SENSE.
BREATHE.

THWWWP

SHOW-OFF.
IF ***I*** HAD SUPER-POWERS--
I KNOW, MJ. WE ALL KNOW.

DON'T STEAL!
WHY IS THAT HARD?
DON'T TAKE THINGS--COME BACK HERE!
PLEASE DON'T!
DON'T TAKE THINGS THAT DON'T BELONG TO YOU!
THIS SHOULDN'T BE HARD!
WHY...
...WHY IS THIS SO HARD?

SHE'S OUT OF CONTROL.
SHE'S NOT A HERO. SHE'S A MONSTER.

SHE CAME... SHE CAME OUTTA NOWHERE.
JUST STARTED SWINGING, YOU KNOW?

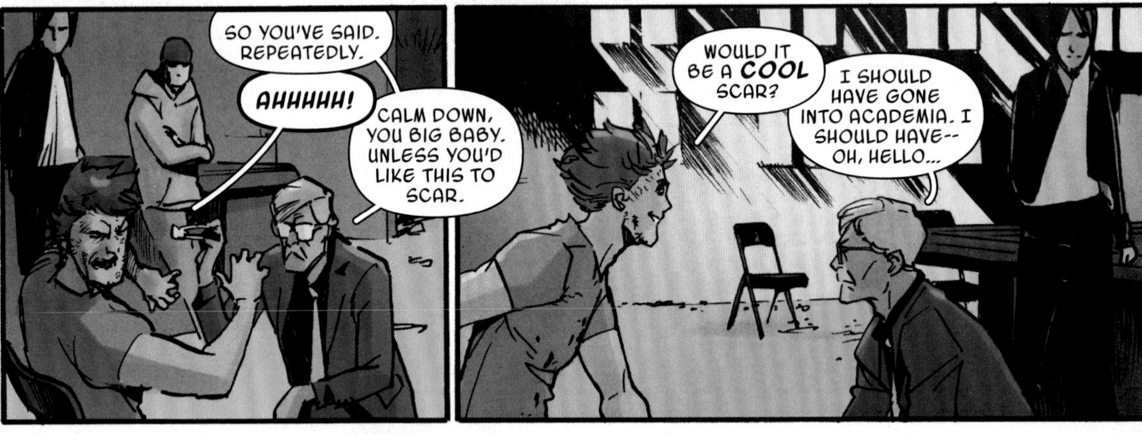
SO YOU'VE SAID. REPEATEDLY.
AHHHHH!
CALM DOWN, YOU BIG BABY. UNLESS YOU'D LIKE THIS TO SCAR.
WOULD IT BE A COOL SCAR?
I SHOULD HAVE GONE INTO ACADEMIA. I SHOULD HAVE-- OH, HELLO...

...HOLD STILL.
I DIDN'T MOVE.

I WASN'T TALKING TO YOU.

KNOCK KNOCK
COME IN, IF YOU'RE WILLING TO RISK IT.

I AM.
REALLY, SCAVENGER?
I THINK YOU'LL WANT TO SEE WHAT I'VE MANAGED TO SCAVENGE THIS TIME.

WHERE DID YOU GET THIS?
PULLED IT OUT OF JACKSON.
THEY'RE CONNECTED TO HER POWERS SOMEHOW. WE HAVE A PIECE OF HER NOW.

I AGREE.
FINISH IT.
ME? BUT I--

YES, YOU.
IT'S TIME TO PROVE THAT YOU'RE A PREDATOR.
IT'S TIME TO KILL THE SPIDER-WOMAN.

THOSE MEN--I HIT THEM TOO HARD.
STUPID. STUPID. YOU'RE A HERO, REMEMBER?

A HERO.

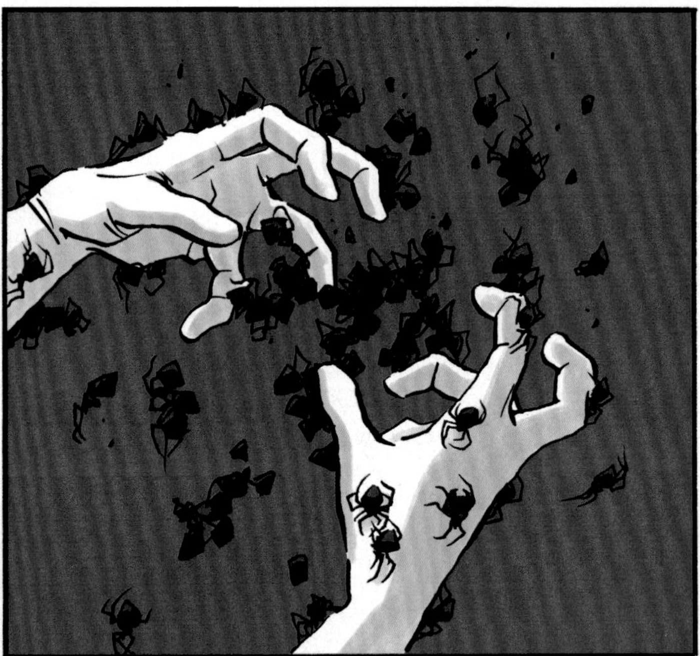

WHY DOES EVERYTHING HAVE TO BE SO HARD?

CURRENTS

FACE IT TIGER
YOU'VE HIT THE
JACKPOT!
I'M HERE!

I'M **ON TIME!**
WOULD YOU LIKE A MEDAL?
SOME LIGHT APPLAUSE MAYBE.
WHERE ARE MJ AND BETTY?
EITHER FIXING THEIR HAIR OR HOOKING UP IN THE GREENROOM. EITHER WAY, SAFER OUT HERE.

NOT MUCH SAFER IF YOU DON'T GET DRESSED.
DON'T WORRY. I'VE GOT THAT COVERED.

SHOW-OFF.
YES.
YOU READY?

I THINK I AM, YEAH. I STILL REMEMBER THE BEAT.
IT'S JUST ONE... TWO...
ONE-TWO-THREE-FOUR!
I DON'T REALLY CARE ABOUT YOUR--
FEELINGS!
GOT NO TIME FOR ALL YOUR DOUBLE--
DEALINGS!
I'M ALL OUT OF PATIENCE FOR YOUR--
DRAMA!
WHY DON'T YOU GO AHEAD AND CRY TO--
MAMA!
MARY JANES
OH OH OH
DO YOU REALLY WANNA GO GO GO
BECAUSE I OUGHT TO WARN YOU, BOY
YOU'RE NOT GOING TO ENJOY THIS FIGHT!

LISTEN... I SAY ... YOU'RE NOT GONNA GET AWAY WAY WAY FROM YOUR ...IGHT--
OH NO. THIS IS NOT THE TIME FOR SPIDER-SENSE.
MJ IS GOING TO KILL ME.
I DON'T SEE ANY--
THERE'S NO JUSTICE THERE'S JUST US SO DON'T MAKE A FUSS IT'S THE ONLY CONCLUSION TO YOUR WEIRD DELUSION.
NO.
GWEN, WHAT THE HELL?!
MOVE!
LOOK! IT'S SPIDER-WOMAN!
WHAT'S SPIDER-WOMAN DOING HERE?
GIVE ME MY PHONE!
YEAH!

OH NO. OH NO.
THEY THINK IT'S ALL PART OF THE SHOW.
CAN'T TELL THEM TO RUN-- THAT'LL ONLY MAKE THINGS WORSE.

WHAT THE--
HEY!

EXPLOSIVES DON'T CARE WHO'S AN INNOCENT BYSTANDER. THEY TAKE US ALL OUT.
PLEASE WORK.

PLEASE WORK.

PLEASE, PLEASE WORK.

...IT DIDN'T WORK.
HARRY, YOU'VE GOT TO--
BOOM

WH...
WHAT...
WHAT *HAPPENED?*
THE BAND AND I WERE JUST PLAYING A GIG, AND NOW--NOW--
EVERYTHING HURTS.
EVERYTHING...
OH, NO.
PLEASE, NO.

THE BAND. HAVE TO FIND...THE BAND.
AND HARRY. I CAN'T...
AHHHHH.
THE HEADACHE ISN'T FROM THE BOMBING. IT'S JUST A HEADACHE.
I SHOULD HAVE BEEN FASTER. I SHOULD HAVE NOTICED--
I SHOULD HAVE SEEN THIS.
I SHOULD HAVE SEEN IT COMING.
HELLO?
IS ANYONE THERE?
...GWEN?
GWEN, WHAT THE HELL? WHAT HAPPENED?
ARE YOU HURT?
NO, JUST PISSED. WHAT DID YOU DO?
HOLD ON, OKAY? I NEED TO HELP EVERYONE ELSE. SO JUST...

JUST HOLD ON.

SHORTLY, OUTSIDE.
CURRENTS

GWEN!
I'M SORRY, SIR, YOU CAN'T-- CAPTAIN?
MY DAUGHTER'S BAND WAS IN THERE!
POLICE LINE DO NOT CROSS POLICE LINE DO NOT CR

GWEN'S BEEN AN INCREDIBLE HELP, SIR. SHE AND THE GIRLS ARE FINE.
WHERE IS SHE?
SHE'S INSIDE THE BUILDING WITH THE SEARCH AND RESCUE TEAMS.
WHAT? SHE'S A CIVILIAN! SHE'S NOT TRAINED--

PLEASE. PLEASE, I NEED SOME HELP HERE!

PLEASE.
PLEASE HELP HIM.

PLEASE, HE'S HURT.
YOU HAVE TO HELP HIM.

FIRST PETER, THEN BILLY...NOW HARRY.
WHY DOES THIS KEEP HAPPENING?

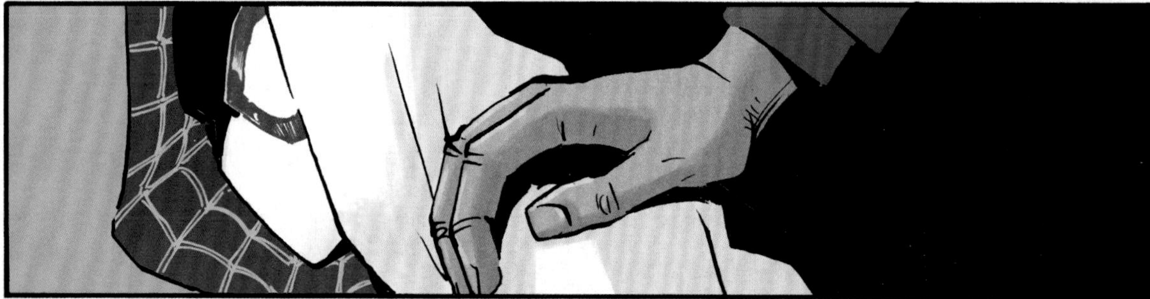

ARE YOU HURT?
THANK GOD.
NO.
BUT SOMEONE'S ABOUT TO BE.
GWEN--

THWP
DON'T WAIT UP.

GWEN!

THIS WASN'T A COINCIDENCE.
SOMEONE TARGETED ME. SOMEONE WENT AFTER MY FAMILY.

I WAS WORRIED ABOUT SWINGING THROUGH THE MULTIVERSE BECAUSE NO ONE WOULD BE ABLE TO TELL MY FAMILY IF I DIED.
I SHOULD HAVE BEEN WORRYING ABOUT THEM.

BUT WHO WOULD WANT TO HURT ME LIKE THIS?
CINDY MOON, MURDOCK, THE HAND...THEY'RE ALL LOCKED UP OR M.I.A.

THOSE JERKS IN THE PARKING LOT THE OTHER DAY.
THEY WERE LAYING A TRAP FOR ME.*
*SEE EXCITING ISSUE #6!

ELSA BROCK WOULDN'T DO THIS.
SO WHO...?

THWWP
NONE OF MY LOCAL SUPER VILLAINS USE BOMBS. I'M NOT LOOKING FOR A SUPER VILLAIN.
I'M LOOKING FOR A MONSTER.

THIS IS WHERE THEY ATTACKED ME.

FOCUS.
IF THEY COULD LAY A TRAP FOR ME HERE, I CAN FOLLOW IT BACK TO THEM. SPIDERS *READ* WEBS.

THE SPIDERS THAT MAKE UP MY COSTUME CAN FIND THINGS FOR ME.
PURSES, CATS... LITTLE THINGS.

THWWP
IF THEY CAN DO THAT, THEY CAN FIND THE PEOPLE WHO DID THIS.

PARK

THE COAST LOOKS CLEAR.

NO SMOKING
THAT GANG WEARS A CRESCENT MOON INSIGNIA.
SOMEONE HAS TO KNOW SOMETHING.
(DO OTHER SUPER HEROES HAVE TO SNEAK AROUND LIKE THIS?)

THIS IS *SO* ILLEGAL. THIS IS *SO* IMPORTANT.

DAD'S PASSWORD SHOULD STILL WORK, AND THEN--
YOU WANT TO STOP RIGHT THERE.
...CRUD.

WHAT DO YOU THINK YOU'RE DOING?
I CAN EXPLAIN.
BECAUSE IT LOOKS LIKE YOU'RE PREPARING TO BREAK INTO A POLICE COMPUTER. WHICH, I THINK YOU KNOW, WOULD BE ILLEGAL.

UM.
TECHNICALLY, THIS IS A PUBLIC BUILDING. TECHNICALLY, YOU HAVEN'T DONE ANYTHING WRONG.
WHY ARE YOU HERE, GWEN?

SOMEONE TARGETED ME AND HURT MY FRIENDS.
I THINK I KNOW WHO IT WAS, BUT...I NEED MORE INFORMATION.

SO YOU CAME HERE BECAUSE YOU WANT TO BEAT THE @#$& OUT OF SOMEBODY?

I CAME HERE BECAUSE SOMEONE HAS TO BRING THEM TO JUSTICE.
I WANT THEM BEHIND BARS.
WHATEVER'S LEFT OF THEM, ANYWAY. BUT I CAN'T SAY THAT TO A COP.

GREAT. WHAT DO YOU KNOW?
THEY ALL WEAR THIS CRESCENT MOON INSIGNIA.
GOT IT.

"THAT'S THE SIGN OF A GUY WHO CALLS HIMSELF 'THE MAN-WOLF.'
"NO ONE'S SURE WHERE HE CAME FROM. HE CROPPED UP WHILE YOU WERE...GONE.
"HE'S BAD NEWS. YOU REALLY SHOULDN'T BE GOING OUT THERE ALONE."
I NEVER GO ANYWHERE ALONE.
ANY OF YOU SEE THE PEOPLE WITH THE MOON BADGES?
UH-HUH. GOOD TO KNOW.
LET'S GO.
IT'S TIME WE FINISH THIS.

HELLO!
WHAM

I NEED SOME HELP, AND YOU LOOK LIKE HELPFUL GENTLEMEN!
WHO WANTS TO TELL ME WHAT I WANT TO KNOW?

THWAP
THWAP

SIGH
THAT'S WHAT I **THOUGHT** YOU'D SAY.
OW!
OOF!

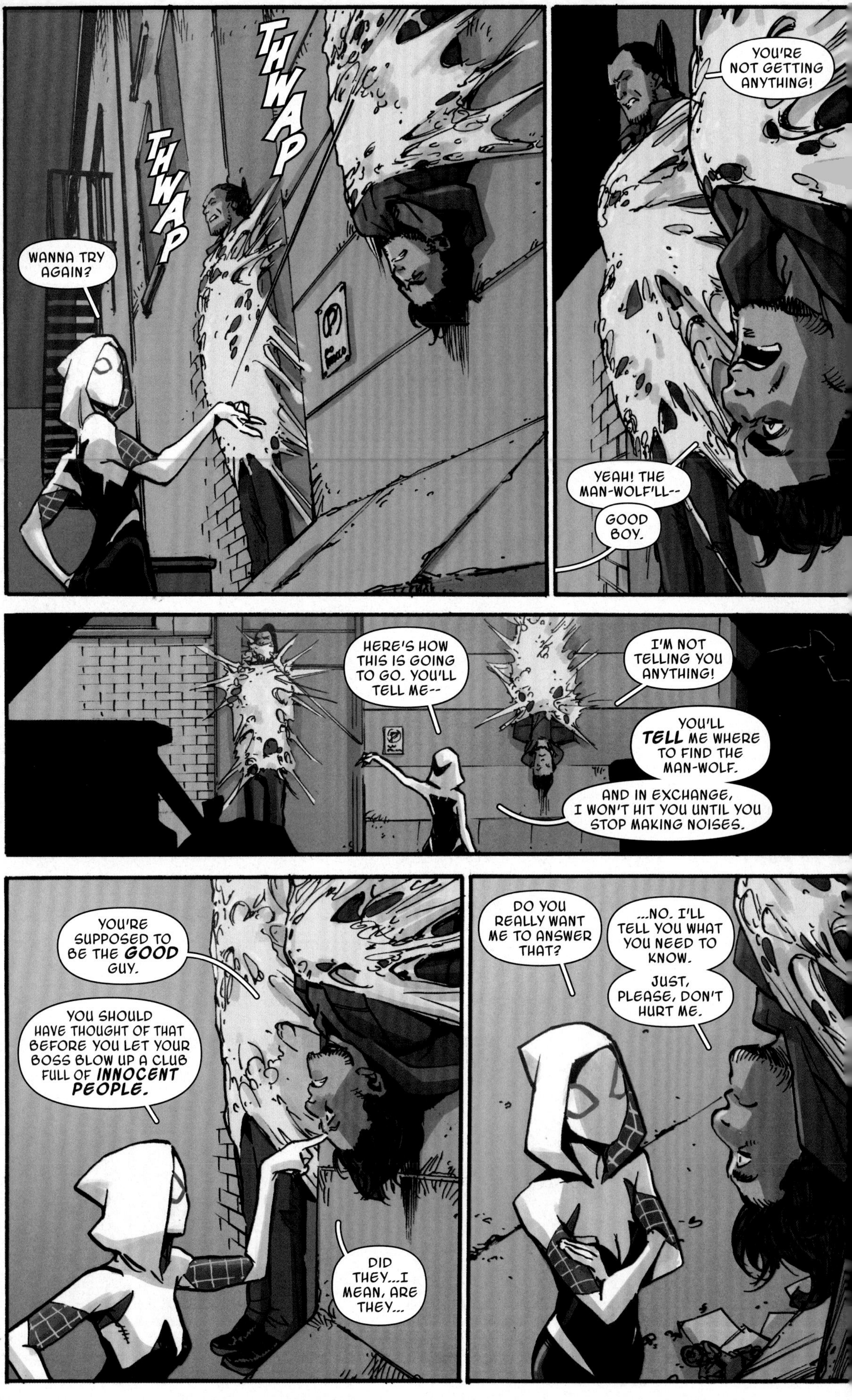

THWAP
THWAP
WANNA TRY AGAIN?
YOU'RE NOT GETTING ANYTHING!
YEAH! THE MAN-WOLF'LL--
GOOD BOY.

YOU'RE SUPPOSED TO BE THE GOOD GUY.
YOU SHOULD HAVE THOUGHT OF THAT BEFORE YOU LET YOUR BOSS BLOW UP A CLUB FULL OF INNOCENT PEOPLE.
DID THEY...I MEAN, ARE THEY...
DO YOU REALLY WANT ME TO ANSWER THAT?
...NO. I'LL TELL YOU WHAT YOU NEED TO KNOW.
JUST, PLEASE, DON'T HURT ME.

HURT HIM? I'M THE HERO.
I DON'T HURT PEOPLE.

WE'RE JUST GOING TO HAVE A CONVERSATION WITH OUR FISTS.
YOU KNOW, LIKE THE GROWN-UPS DO.

BIG, EMPTY, CREEPY WAREHOUSES. THOSE ARE NEVER BAD, RIGHT?
I'M SURE EVERYBODY'S OUT BUYING NEW CURTAINS FOR THEIR SEASONAL SPRUCE-UP.

ALL RIGHT, TIME TO SEARCH THE PLA--

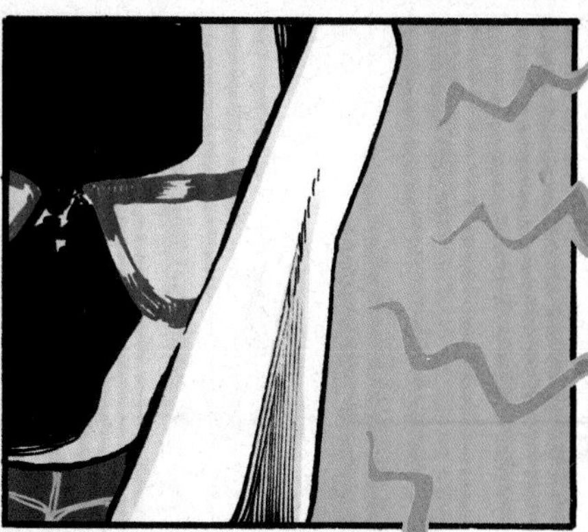

WE SAY HELLO WITH WORDS, NOT HANDS!

YOU HURT MY--
OH. OH MY GOD.

HELLO, LITTLE GIRL.
DECIDED TO BAIT THE BEAST IN HIS DEN, DID YOU?

I NEVER THOUGHT YOU'D BE THIS **FOOLISH.**

I THINK I SPEAK FOR EVERYONE HERE WHEN I SAY WHAT THE **HELL.**
SAYS THE SPIDER.
IT'S A GIMMICK, NOT A FURSONA.

I COULD HAVE GONE WITH "SUPER-AWESOME-WOMAN," BUT IT FELT LIKE BRAGGING.
SO APART FROM THE OBVIOUS, **WHAT** IS YOUR **PROBLEM?**

ISN'T IT OBVIOUS, SPIDER-BRAT?

YOU ARE!
OWWWWWWWWW!

YOU THINK THIS IS YOUR CITY?
YOU THINK THIS IS A GAME?
GET UP. GET UP. GET UP. GET UP.
GET UP NOW.

AHHHHHHH!
BETTER HEROES THAN YOU HAVE TRIED, LITTLE GIRL.

I SLEEP IN A BED OF THEIR BONES.

SNRK.
HEH. HA HA HA--

ARE YOU LAUGHING? WHY ARE YOU LAUGHING?
"A BED OF THEIR BONES"? SERIOUSLY?
WHAT ARE YOU, TWELVE?

WHAM
YEAH, YOU HURT ME. WHATEVER. COMES WITH THE JOB.
I CAN TAKE IT.

YOU HURT MY FRIENDS?
SCREW YOU.
SCREW YOU FOREVER.

THWWP

I NEED TO GET OUT OF HERE.
I'M HURT BAD.
BUT THIS ENDS HERE. NOW.

I'M TOO ANGRY TO HOLD BACK LIKE I NORMALLY WOULD. I CAN LIFT CARS. IF I PUNCHED AN ORDINARY PERSON WITHOUT RESTRAINING MYSELF, I'D TAKE THEIR HEAD OFF.
WELL, HE STILL HAS A HEAD. BUT HE'LL WISH HE DIDN'T IN THE MORNING.
YIPE!

BAD DOG. STAY DOWN.

SLAM
RRRRRRAAAARR--

YOU WANT TO KNOW WHY THIS IS MY CITY?
YOU WANT TO KNOW WHY I WIN AND YOU LOSE?

BECAUSE I'M NOT A MONSTER.
THWWP
BECAUSE I'M NEVER GOING TO BE.

DON'T YOU WANT TO KNOW MY SECRET? MY **STORY?**
DON'T YOU WANT TO KNOW HOW I BECAME A **GOD?**

THWAP
LOTS OF TIME FOR STORIES WHILE YOU'RE IN CUSTODY.

I NEED TO GET BACK TO THE HOSPITAL.
BUT IF YOU EVER COME NEAR ANYONE I LOVE AGAIN, YOU'LL WISH I'D BEEN A MONSTER.
MONSTERS **END** THINGS.

HI, DAD?
I NEED SOME OFFICERS WITH REALLY BIG HANDCUFFS--

--AND MAYBE A DOGCATCHER'S VAN.
I'LL GIVE YOU THE ADDRESS.

LATER.
HOSPITAL
HEY. SORRY IT TOOK ME SO LONG TO GET HERE.
I CAME AS FAST AS I COULD.
THIS IS MINE. I OWN THIS.
EVEN AFTER EVERYTHING, DEATH STILL LOVES GWEN STACY.
GWEN?
I KNEW YOU'D SHOW UP SOONER OR LATER.
I'M... I'M SO SORRY.
YOU SHOULD BE. YOU WERE RUSHING THE BEAT AGAIN.
HEH.
WE'RE HERE.
YEAH. WE ARE.
WE ALL ARE.
DEATH LOVES GWEN STACY. GWEN STACY LOVES HER *PEOPLE*.

10

"YOU CAN'T STOP THE BEAT"

OKAY. HERE'S THE SKINNY.
MY NAME'S GWEN STACY. I WAS BITTEN BY A RADIOACTIVE SPIDER, WHICH GAVE ME SUPER-POWERS.
THEN, THE WOMAN WHO ARRANGED FOR THE SPIDER'S CREATION TOOK MY POWERS AWAY FROM ME AND STARTED SLIPPING ME SPECIAL ISOTOPES TO LET ME KEEP BEING SPIDER-WOMAN.
ONLY I SURPRISED EVERYONE BY BONDING TO A LAB-GROWN GOO THAT WAS SUPPOSED TO KILL ME, AND NOW I GET MY POWERS FROM IT.

STAY. THE POLICE WILL BE HERE SOON.
YOU CAN'T DO--

GO AHEAD. FINISH THAT SENTENCE.
YEAH, I DIDN'T THINK SO.

NOW THE TROUBLE IS, I THINK SOMETHING'S WRONG WITH THE THING THAT GIVES ME MY POWERS.
I'VE BEEN HAVING HEADACHES. BAD ONES.
AND I'M DROPPING GUMMY SPIDERS EVERYWHERE I GO.

DR. ELSA BROCK MADE THE GUMMY SPIDERS THAT GIVE ME MY POWERS, BUT SHE'S GONE MISSING.
NO ONE HAS ANY IDEA WHERE SHE IS.

FORTUNATELY, THANKS TO A PARALLEL-UNIVERSE VERSION OF MYSELF WHO CREATED DIMENSION-HOPPING TECH FOR ME WHEN I WAS STRANDED IN HER WORLD, I HAVE OTHER OPTIONS.

FWOOP
WHEN ANSWERS AREN'T AVAILABLE LOCALLY, I CAN GO LOOKING ELSEWHERE.

EARTH-616. HOME OF PETER PARKER, THE AMAZING SPIDER-MAN.
FWOOP

BWOOOOOM

AHHHHHHH!
THIS WILL NEVER NOT BE DISCONCERTING!

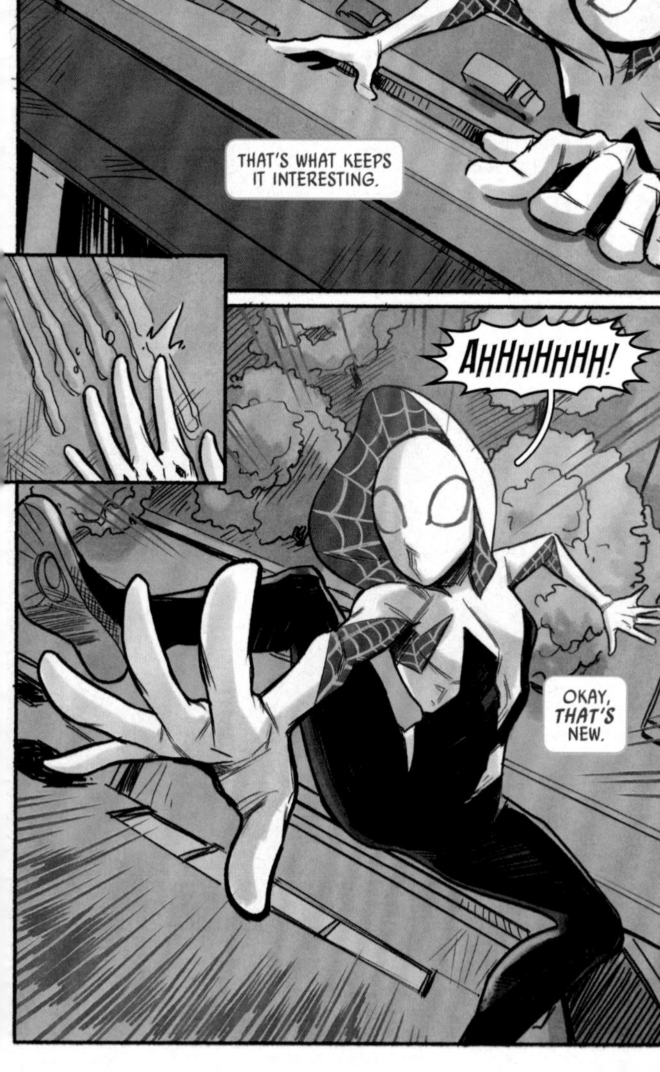
BUT I THINK PAN-DIMENSIONAL TRAVEL *SHOULD* BE A LITTLE DISCONCERTING.
THAT'S WHAT KEEPS IT INTERESTING.
AHHHHHHH!
OKAY, *THAT'S* NEW.

POWERS, NOT WORKING.
TIMING, INCONVENIENT.

OKAY. **WHY** POWERS NOT WORKING?

THEORY: WEB OF LIFE AND DESTINY DAMAGED. I HAVEN'T BEEN TRAVELING IN A WHILE. MAYBE WITHOUT THE WEB, THINGS AREN'T SYNCHRONIZING RIGHT.

HMMM.

COSTUME ISN'T RESPONDING, EITHER.

LOOKS LIKE MY ORIGINAL *"SWING AROUND AND FIND PETER"* PLAN IS ON HOLD, AND I'M STROLLING THROUGH MANHATTAN IN SPANDEX.

(UGH.)

UNLESS THIS IS A COMPLETELY *FERAL* PARALLEL DIMENSION, THEY'LL HAVE INTERNET AT THE LIBRARY.
MILES AND PETER ARE REASONABLY FUNCTIONAL, SO THERE MUST BE SOME CIVILIZATION HERE.

OKAY, LET'S DO THIS.
TIME FOR SOME...

...RESEARCH!

PLAGIARISM?
REALLY, PETER?*
AT LEAST IT LOOKS LIKE HE'S A T.A. AT EMPIRE STATE UNIVERSITY NOW. BOUNCING BACK.
TAPPA TAPPA TAP
*CHECK OUT AMAZING SPIDER-MAN (2018) VOL. 1 --DEVIN

I GUESS I KNOW WHERE I'LL START.
STICKY POWERS ARE WORKING AGAIN--FOR NOW AT LEAST.
NEXT STOP, *EMPIRE STATE UNIVERSITY,* HOME TO A CERTAIN...

...SPIDER-MAN.
FOR THE RECORD, I ONLY WORK AT ESU. I DON'T LIVE THERE.
SPIDER-MAN!
NOT SPIDER-MAN! WHAT ARE YOU DOING HERE? I THOUGHT YOU WERE TAKING A BREAK.
I AM. HOW DID YOU FIND ME?
I SET UP A DETECTOR FOR INTERDIMENSIONAL PORTALS, AND YOU'RE LEAVING A NICE TRAIL OF PARTICLES FROM EARTH-65.
I'VE BEEN UP HERE FOR, LIKE, AN HOUR. WHAT TOOK YOU SO LONG?
I HAD TO WALK FROM CENTRAL PARK.
I'VE BEEN HAVING TROUBLE WITH MY POWERS, AND THEY REALLY DIDN'T SEEM TO LIKE TRANSITIONING INTO YOUR UNIVERSE.
WHY DID YOU START OUT BY GOING TO THE LIBRARY?
I COULDN'T SHOW YOUR LOCAL NERDS MY PHONE, AND IT'S NOT LIKE I HAVE YOUR ADDRESS.

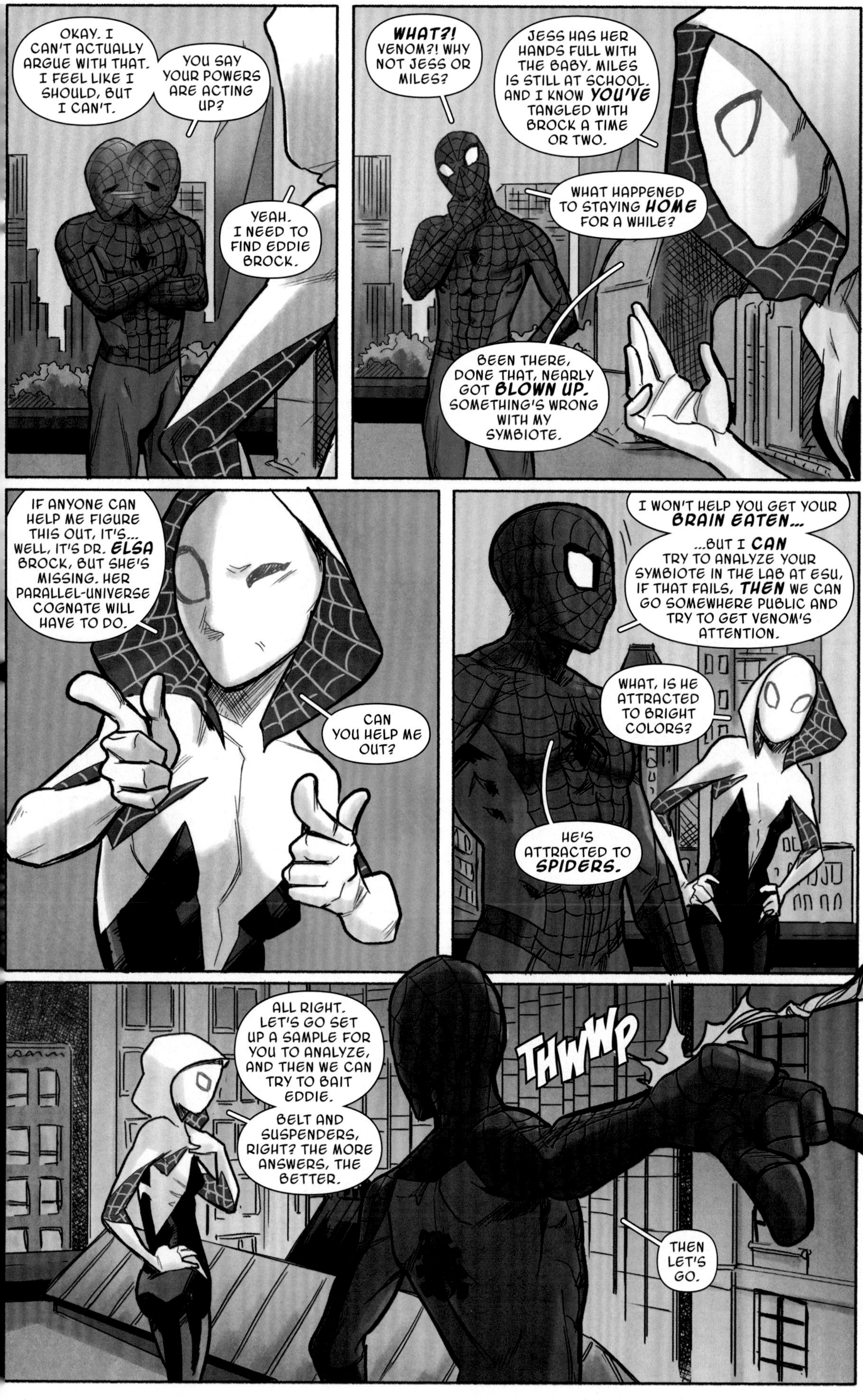

OKAY. I CAN'T ACTUALLY ARGUE WITH THAT. I FEEL LIKE I SHOULD, BUT I CAN'T.
YOU SAY YOUR POWERS ARE ACTING UP?
YEAH. I NEED TO FIND EDDIE BROCK.
WHAT?! VENOM?! WHY NOT JESS OR MILES?
JESS HAS HER HANDS FULL WITH THE BABY. MILES IS STILL AT SCHOOL. AND I KNOW YOU'VE TANGLED WITH BROCK A TIME OR TWO.
WHAT HAPPENED TO STAYING HOME FOR A WHILE?
BEEN THERE, DONE THAT, NEARLY GOT BLOWN UP. SOMETHING'S WRONG WITH MY SYMBIOTE.
IF ANYONE CAN HELP ME FIGURE THIS OUT, IT'S... WELL, IT'S DR. ELSA BROCK, BUT SHE'S MISSING. HER PARALLEL-UNIVERSE COGNATE WILL HAVE TO DO.
CAN YOU HELP ME OUT?
I WON'T HELP YOU GET YOUR BRAIN EATEN...
...BUT I CAN TRY TO ANALYZE YOUR SYMBIOTE IN THE LAB AT ESU, IF THAT FAILS, THEN WE CAN GO SOMEWHERE PUBLIC AND TRY TO GET VENOM'S ATTENTION.
WHAT, IS HE ATTRACTED TO BRIGHT COLORS?
HE'S ATTRACTED TO SPIDERS.
ALL RIGHT. LET'S GO SET UP A SAMPLE FOR YOU TO ANALYZE, AND THEN WE CAN TRY TO BAIT EDDIE.
BELT AND SUSPENDERS, RIGHT? THE MORE ANSWERS, THE BETTER.
THWWP
THEN LET'S GO.

SHORTLY.
WOO!
HOO!
I'VE MISSED THIS. STAYING HOME WAS THE RIGHT CALL, BUT THERE'S NOTHING LIKE SHARING THE WIND WITH SOMEONE WHO HAS THEIR OWN WEB-LINE TO HOLD ON TO. I NEED OTHER SPIDERS.
I BROKE MY PROMISE NOT TO TRAVEL BETWEEN DIMENSIONS FOR THEM. THE LEAST THEY COULD DO IS STAY WITH ME WHILE I TRY TO FIX THEM.
I'LL NEED YOU TO COME BACK NEXT WEEK FOR THE RESULTS ON THE SPIDERS YOU GIVE ME.
CHECK. THEY CAN LIVE A LONG TIME SEPARATED FROM THE REST OF MY SUIT.
DO THEY HAVE TO EAT?
YES.

BZZBZZZBZZ
HM?
DANGER? BUT WHERE?
NO ONE'S SCREAMING, AND I DON'T SEE ANYTHING.
I JUST NEED TO BE CAREFUL.
YO! DID YOU FEEL THAT?
FEEL WHAT?
I'D REALLY APPRECIATE IT IF MY POWERS WOULD GET THEIR ACT TOGETHER.
AHHHH!
GWEN?!
I TOLD YOU SOMETHING WAS WRONG. IT MOSTLY MANIFESTS AS HEADACHES.
EATING USUALLY HELPS. THE SUIT BURNS A LOT OF CALORIES.
IS THERE SOMEPLACE HERO-FRIENDLY WHERE WE CAN STOP?

COME ON. THERE'S AN EXCELLENT HOT DOG CART DOWN THIS WAY.
GOOD. I NEED TO EAT SOMETHING BEFORE I KEEL OVER.
PAP
THUMP

AND THERE'S A CHANCE THIS GETS EDDIE TO COME OUT OF HIDING.
BEAUTIFUL DAY, CENTRAL PARK...THIS IS LIKE CATNIP FOR SUPER VILLAINS.
THIS JOB NEVER GETS MORE LOGICAL, DOES IT?

UGH, REALLY?
WHAT'S UP?
I THINK MY SPIDER-SENSE IS STILL BUSTED. SO WHAT'S THIS ABOUT PLAGIARISM?
BZZZZZZ

UM. DOC OCK TOOK OVER MY BODY FOR A WHILE, AND HE FINISHED MY DEGREE WHILE HE WAS IN THERE.* TECHNICALLY, SINCE HIS WORK WAS PUBLISHED UNDER MY NAME, IT'S PLAGIARISM. I GUESS. THE LAW DOESN'T ACCOUNT FOR EXCHANGE OF CONSCIOUSNESS.
WHAT.
OH, LOOK! THAT HOT DOG STAND I TOLD YOU ABOUT!
*SEE SUPERIOR SPIDER-MAN FOR THE DEETS! --DANNY

YOU COME BACK HERE, SPIDER-MAN.
WE NEED TO TALK ABOUT THIS.

CAN'T TALK NOW, TOO HUNGRY!
I NEED HOT DOGS TO LIVE!

GOOD OLD-FASHIONED MEAT TUBES.
DO YOU HAVE THESE WHERE YOU COME FROM?

EVERYONE HAS HOT DOGS.
(WELL, MAYBE NOT SPIDER-HAM.)
THEY'RE UNIVERSAL. EVEN IF THEY ARE INFERIOR TO CORN DOGS. I'LL TAKE TWO.

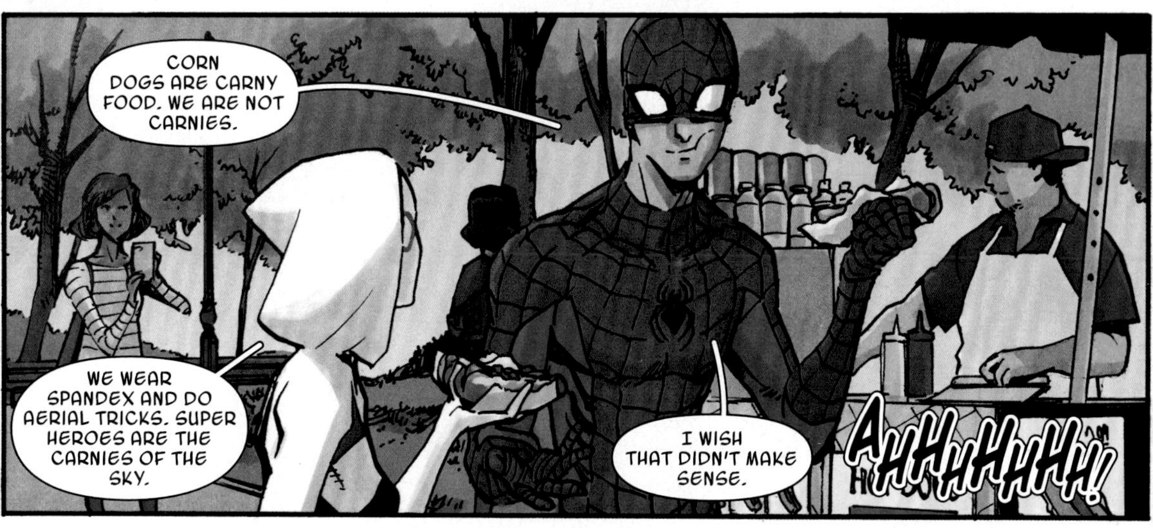
CORN DOGS ARE CARNY FOOD. WE ARE NOT CARNIES.
WE WEAR SPANDEX AND DO AERIAL TRICKS. SUPER HEROES ARE THE CARNIES OF THE SKY.
I WISH THAT DIDN'T MAKE SENSE.
AHHHHHHHH!

WHAT IS THAT?
AHHHHHHHH!
SOMETHING'S REALLY WRONG!
IT'S COMING FROM THE MUSEUM!

AHHHHHHHH!
HOW ARE YOU STILL HOLDING THOSE HOT DOGS?
I'M HUNGRY!
THWWP

I DON'T SEE ANYTHING.
I CAN SEE THE DINOSAURS!
OH, DON'T SAY TH--

--AT. DON'T SAY THAT.
DON'T YOU HAVE SWARM IN YOUR WORLD?
WHAT THE-- BEES. IT'S ALL BEES. HOW IS IT ALL BEES?
NOW YOU'RE JUST MESSING WITH ME.
ALL SHALL COWER BEFORE THE TERRIBLE PREHISTORIC GLORY OF THE
DINOSWARM!
HIS NAME IS FRITZ VON MEYER. HE WAS A NAZI SCIENTIST. NOW HE'S A SUPER VILLAIN.
A SUPER VILLAIN MADE OF BEES.
WAIT. HE'S A WHOLE SWARM OF BEES? DOES HE MAKE HONEY? DOES HE MAKE BABY BEES WITH HIMSELF?
TO BE HONEST, I'VE NEVER LOOKED TOO DEEPLY INTO THE BIOLOGY.
SWARM CAN FORM AROUND SKELETONS. THE MUSEUM IS DISPLAYING ONE OF THE FEW COMPLETE UTAHRAPTOR OSTROMMAYSORUM SKELETONS. IT'S NOT A REPLICA. THAT MUST BE WHY HE'S STEALING IT.
WHY BE JUST A SWARM OF NAZI BEES WHEN YOU CAN BE A SWARM OF NAZI DINOSAUR BEES?
PRECISELY.
THIS IS MAKING MY HEAD HURT.
WANT TO GO PUNCH SOME BEES?
DESPERATELY.
THAT'S THE SPIRIT!

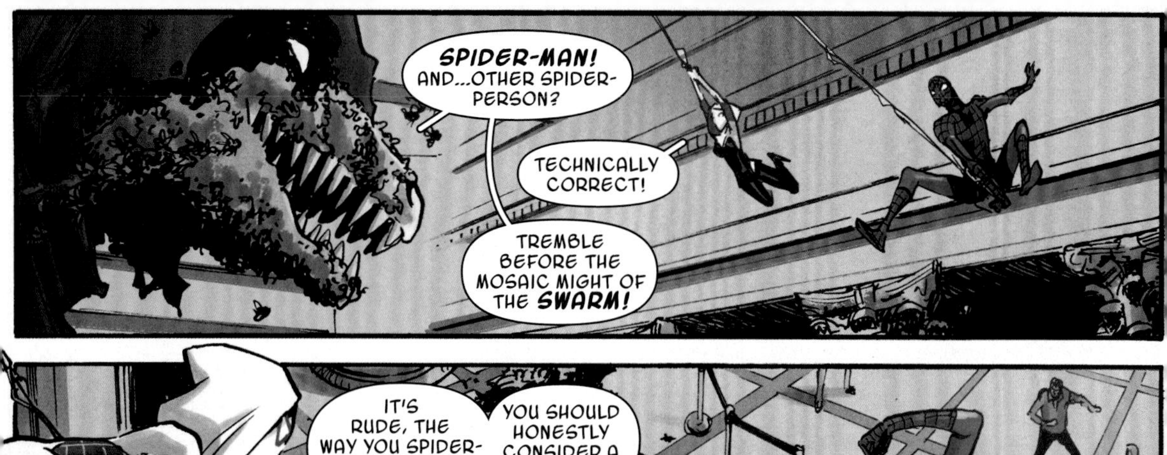
SPIDER-MAN! AND...OTHER SPIDER-PERSON?
TECHNICALLY CORRECT!
TREMBLE BEFORE THE MOSAIC MIGHT OF THE SWARM!

IT'S RUDE, THE WAY YOU SPIDER-PEOPLE KEEP INCREASING.
YOU SHOULD HONESTLY CONSIDER A REGISTRY.
YOU'RE STEALING FOSSILS FROM A MUSEUM! YOU DON'T GET TO TALK ABOUT RUDENESS!
PSST. HOW DO WE PUNCH BEES?
ENTHUSIASTICALLY!

FOOLISH HEROES! DO YOU THINK I'M ONLY STEALING FOSSILS?
OOF! YOU'RE STEALING AT LEAST ONE.
MUSEUMS ARE FULL OF SMALL, VALUABLE ITEMS. BEES HAVE SURPRISING LIFTING CAPACITY.
I'M STEALING WHATEVER I WANT!

NOPE.
INSOLENT BRAT!
BEE-PUNCHING TIME.

PUNCHING NAZI BEES IS EVEN BETTER THAN PUNCHING REGULAR NAZIS!
ROAR!
MIND THE POINTY ENDS!

ROAR!
BUZZZZZZZZZZZZZZZZZZZ

SPIDER-MAN! WE NEED TO CONTAIN HIM!
LITTLE BUSY HERE.
SO MANY BEES...

PREHISTORIC PREDATOR PARTY
IT'S LIKE MAKING A CORN DOG.
WE'LL GET YOU ANOTHER HOT DOG.
YOU NEED TO WRAP THE MEAT COMPLETELY.

OH NO. NO, THIS IS NOT THE TIME FOR A POWER FAILURE.

GOOD SYMBIOTE. VERY, VERY GOOD SYMBIOTE. I'LL EAT A DOZEN CORN DOGS FOR YOU WHEN WE GET HOME.

ALMOST... GOT...IT.
THWWP

UNHAND ME!
BZZZZZZZ

OOOWWWWWWW!
I CANNOT BE CONTAINED!
WATCH ME!
THWWP
ROAR!!
THWWP
THWWP
BUZZZZZ

THAT SHOULD HOLD HIM FOR A WHILE.
LET'S GET THESE PEOPLE OUT OF HERE.
YOU CAN'T STOP ME THIS EASI--

MMMMMMFF! MMMF! MMMF!
THWWP
THWWP
OH, STUFF IT.

SORRY ABOUT THAT.
I KNOW IT'S WEIRD WHEN THE EXHIBITS TRY TO EAT YOU.
IF YOU'D JUST FOLLOW US, WE'LL GET YOU OUT OF HERE.

I'M ALLERGIC TO BEES. I COULD HAVE DIED!
I TOLD YOU NEW YORK WAS FULL OF SUPER VILLAINS.
HEY, SPIDER-MAN, CAN I GET A SELFIE?
I DON'T KNOW YOU. WHO ARE YOU?

I HAVE A SECRET IDENTITY HERE.
CAN'T BE SPIDER-WOMAN. JESSICA WOULD KILL ME.
IT'S TIME TO FINALLY SETTLE ON A NEW CODENAME.

I KEEP SAYING THAT DEATH LOVES GWEN STACY, SO LET'S COMMIT:
YOU CAN CALL ME...GHOST-SPIDER.
GHOST-SPIDER?
ROLL WITH IT, SPIDER-MAN.
YOU SHOULD ALL GET OUTSIDE.
THE POLICE ARE ON THEIR WAY.
SOMEONE'S CALLED THEM BY NOW.
THANK YOU, SPIDER-MAN! THANKS, GHOST-SPIDER!
CAN THE POLICE HOLD A SWARM OF NAZI BEES ATTACHED TO A DINOSAUR SKELETON?
NEW YORK'S FINEST ARE SURPRISINGLY GOOD AT CONTAINING WEIRD SUPER-SCIENCE VILLAINS.
NOT A SKILL SET THE POLICE BACK HOME HAVE HAD TO DEVELOP YET.
WHATEVER'S GOING ON WITH YOUR POWERS... WE'LL FIGURE IT OUT.
AND ABOUT YOUR HOT DOGS...

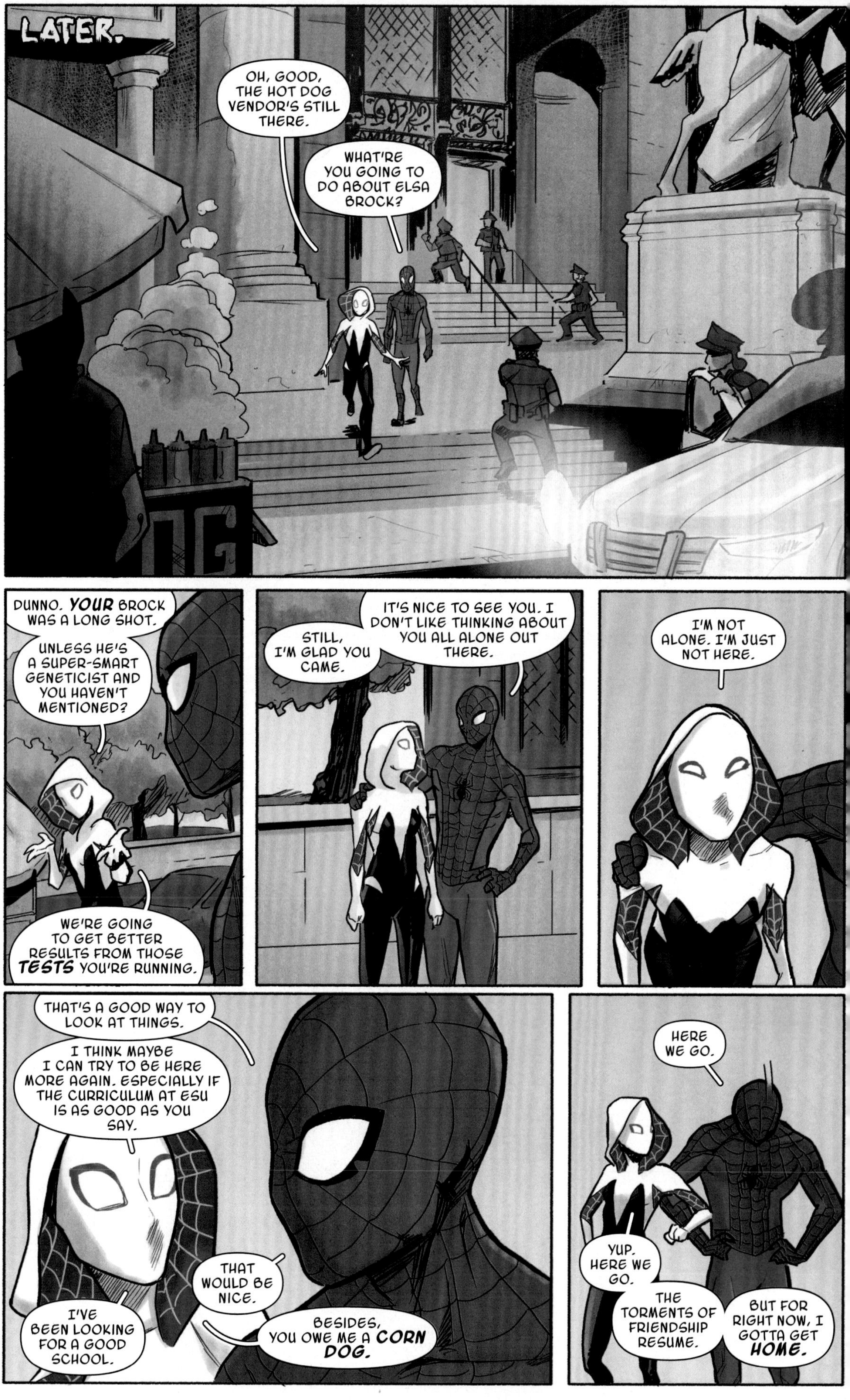

LATER.

OH, GOOD, THE HOT DOG VENDOR'S STILL THERE.

WHAT'RE YOU GOING TO DO ABOUT ELSA BROCK?

EARTH-65.
HOME OF THE HAUNTING
GHOST-SPIDER.
PETER WILL FIGURE OUT WHAT'S WRONG WITH ME.
HE'S ONE OF THE SMARTEST PEOPLE I KNOW.
NIGHTMARE AT THE
AND MAYBE IT'S TIME FOR ME TO REMEMBER JUST HOW OPEN MY OPTIONS REALLY ARE.
SPIDERS DON'T HOLD STILL WHEN THEY HAVE ANY OTHER CHOICE. AND I HAVE ALL THE CHOICES IN THE MULTIVERSE.
TIME TO START MAKING A FEW.

EMBRACE CHANGE

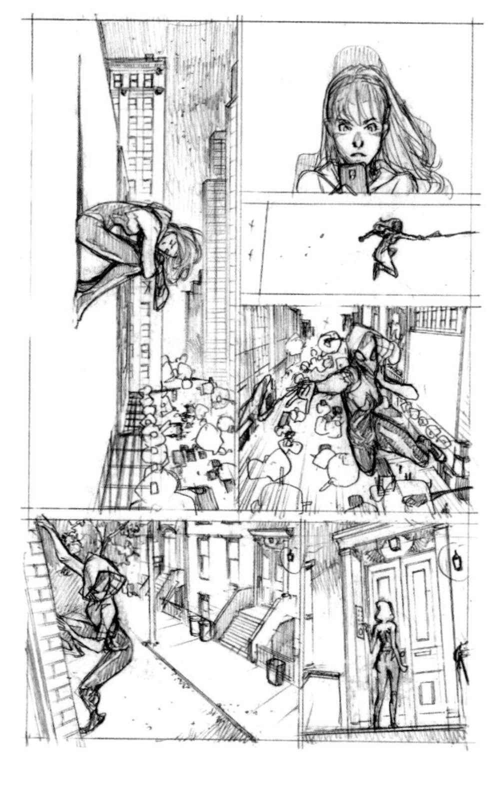

NO LOITERING